Backcountry Skiing
in the
High Sierra

compiled by
John Moynier

D1522266

Chockstone Press, Inc.
Evergreen, Colorado

PUBLISHED AND DISTRIBUTED BY:
Chockstone Press, Inc.
Post Office Box 3505
Evergreen, Colorado 80439

ISBN 0-934641-44-7

Front cover photo: Shredding Sierran snow by Jon Beihoffer.
Back cover photos: Top: Skiing below Bear Creek Spire by John Moynier.
Bottom: A skier in the Wahoo Gully by John Moynier.

WARNING

Backcountry skiing is a potentially hazardous activity. This guide in no way is intended to be a "how to" book. The information contained herein is merely a composite of opinions about where routes go and how difficult they may be. It is a supplement to the user's own knowledge and common sense regarding backcountry skiing and winter hazards, including but not limited to the development of skills needed for safe winter travel, avalanche awareness and rescue techniques, weather-related illnesses and conditions and other pertinent issues. If you are not willing to accept the risks inherent in backcountry skiing, do not use this book. Please use caution when venturing into the backcountry on skis.

ABOUT THE AUTHOR

JOHN MOYNIER HAS MADE HIS LIVING guiding folks on Sierra ski tours for many years. He was chief guide and chief instructor for the Rock Creek Winter Lodge, located in the eastern Sierra, and currently is supervisor for the telemark program at the Mammoth Mountain Ski School. He spends much of his time traveling the west teaching Nordic ski clinics.

John also is a member of the American Association of Avalanche Professionals, serving on the association's backcountry committee. He has taught Nordic skiing in Australia and helped establish the first Nordic ski area in New Zealand, where he guided folks on backcountry ski tours.

John currently is chairman of the Nordic division of the Professional Ski Instructors of America-West and has been both an examiner and clinician for many years.

John also is a mountain guide and a member of the American Mountain Guides Association, serving on its certification and ski mountaineering committees.

Author John Moynier

ACKNOWLEDGMENTS

IF THIS READS LIKE an Academy Awards speech, I apologize, but this book has been very much a community project. I first would like to thank David Beck of Sierra Ski Touring and Doug Robinson for introducing myself and the world to the joys of skiing the Sierra. I particularly would like to thank Dion Goldsworthy, Mark Williams and Janet Rantz for the very special spirit of their Rock Creek Winter Lodge, as well as giving me the chance to live in that wonderful canyon.

I could never thank Allan Bard enough for all his dedication, enthusiasm and patience. Allan and his partners at Alpine Expeditions – Tom Carter, Chris Cox and Kimberly Walker – have been the inspiration for this project. Thanks also to Bela and Mimi Vadasz, Peter Leh and Dave Prudhames of Alpine Skills International for all their help, and especially to Norm Wilson for sharing his tremendous love of skiing and vast knowledge of avalanche awareness.

Special thanks to Dan Asay, Bruce Brossman, Sue Burak, Dori Cann, Will Crljenko, Scott Croll, Michael Graber, Mick Hampton, Jim Harper, Randy Jewitt, Malcolm Jolley, Susan Jordan, Chris Libby, Pete Lewis, Tim Messick, Dennis Oakeshott, Paul Parker, Robert "SP" Parker, Allan Pietrasanta, Michael Pope, Stephen Pope, Galen Rowell, Tom Tuttle, Gordon Wiltsie, James Wilson and all those others who've been patient while I asked stupid questions, fiddled with my camera or hogged first tracks.

I especially would like to thank the following people for providing me with their great knowledge of the Sierra and their fine photography: Allan Bard, Tom Carter, Vern Clevenger, Chris Cox, John Dittli, Chris Falkenstein, Claude Fiddler, Tim Forsell, Dion Goldsworthy, Dave Page, Andy Selters and Jim Stimson. Thanks also to Richard Leversee and the good folks at Black Diamond for providing the ski world with such wonderful backcountry ski equipment. Finally, I would like to thank George Meyers of Chockstone Press for giving life to this project, and Phillips Camera House in Bishop for their fine photo reproductions. Thanks y'all!

This book is dedicated to my parents, Pierre and Ruth Moynier, who encouraged me to pursue a life as an itinerant mountain guide rather than something mundane like a doctor or lawyer.

FOREWORD

The rosy light of dawn drenches the snow-cloaked peaks visible from my kitchen window. Fifteen miles away and ten thousand feet above me, the wind scours the southern slopes and quietly drifts its wind-born harvest into the north-facing bowls. Hot black coffee, the crackle of the wood stove and new snow in the hills promises another memorable day of skiing.

I love this magnificent place, covered in a mantle of fresh snow. It is just possibly the most wonderfully unique mountain range in the world for us backcountry skiing types. Of course, ask anyone (even non-skiers) about California snow and they'll tell you about "Sierra cement." Well, I'm here to tell you something magical happens when those storms climb towards the Sierra Crest: The higher they get, the drier they get. By the time that snow takes up its seasonal residence on the eastside, it is some kind of fabulous fluff. Deep, too. Snow that arguably is as good as "the greatest snow on earth" you've heard of elsewhere.

But even on this morning – crisp with winter – it's not powder that comes to mind when I think of skiing the High Sierra; it's spring corn. If there's one thing we have here in these hills, it's Mother Nature's finest corn snow factory. Mountains with high altitude at a low latitude; sunny California days and freezing mountain nights work to produce a perennial crop of perfect Sierra corn.

Some time ago, some good friends of mine let me in on this little secret and I moved to the eastern Sierra. Great powder in the winter and silky corn snow in the spring; ideal terrain and ideal weather – what more could you ask for? Back then, I was working as a laborer, stocking drywall during the fall, biding my time until winter. Each day I would stare at the crest, wishing the snow would fly to relieve me of that arduous task, so that I might ski free and wild in these marvelous mountains.

Times change. I get a good laugh now thinking about the gear and techniques we used to use. All we knew was that we were having a blast. Still are, in fact. What hasn't changed is that backcountry skiing here still seems like a well-guarded secret. It can't be as good as they say, can it?

Well, for those folks willing to venture into these mountains, the world they'll find is wild and uncrowded. Thousands of square miles of wilderness to live out all of their skiing dreams. I once was told that travelling to the great mountain ranges of the world was an exercise in appreciation for the High Sierra, but I had to find out for myself. I travelled the world in search of exotic skiing experiences, only to find the best skiing right here in my own backyard. Now I know what they meant. Skiing the High Sierra has enriched my life beyond all expectations. May it do the same for you.

ALLAN BARD
BISHOP, CALIFORNIA

PREFACE

THE IDEA FOR THIS BOOK first took hold when I got a copy of the book *Sierra Spring Ski-Touring,* by H.J. Burhenne, which was published in 1971. The stated goal of the book was simple: "One-day tours to 28 peaks." What a great idea! Mr. Burhenne and his friends just wanted to share their favorite trips with the rest of us aspiring backcountry skiers, and give us a few tips along the way.

That book was followed by David Beck's *Ski Touring in California,* published most recently in 1980 and also out-of-print. While both of these books served to whet the skier's appetite, they dealt mostly with day tours and covered the Tahoe area more than the High Sierra. These day tours have been published in various more recent books, but they are a bit of a tease in that they lead you up to timberline, only to turn you back just when you've gotten into the high country.

This book is meant to be an introduction to the skiing potential of the "real" high country: the realm above timberline. I enlisted the help of my friends – most of them have spent much of their adult lives guiding folks on these very tours. We spent many long hours pouring over maps, discussing routes and reminiscing about memorable trips and ski descents, as well as discussing the philosophies of guidebooks such as this. We didn't solve any of the world's great problems, but we had fun working on this project.

In an area as huge as this, there obviously are an infinite number of equally spectacular and challenging routes that I have left out of this book. As with any guidebook, a certain feeling of opening "Pandora's Box" exists, and the temptation to keep some secrets has been very real. It has been my intention to provide an inticing introduction to the range while maintaining the spirit of adventure and discovery. This book is just the tip of the iceberg – I hope it encourages you to explore even further.

There has been a great tradition of guiding people on ski tours in the High Sierra. It is in the spirit of that tradition that I have written this guide. I hope you enjoy reading this book and then get out the maps, put on your skis and discover your own "secret" tours. Happy skiing.

TABLE OF CONTENTS

I.   INTRODUCTION   1
   Getting There   2
   Using this Guide   2
   History   5
   Winter Awareness   7
   Weather   7
   Avalanche   9
   Winter Ecology   18

II.   THE SIERRA CREST   21
   A. Horseshoe Meadows to Kearsarge Pass   23
   B. Kearsarge Pass to South Lake   29
   C. South Lake to North Lake   35
   D. North Lake to Rock Creek   39
   E. Rock Creek to Mammoth Lakes   43
   F. Mammoth Lakes to Tioga Pass   47
   G. Tioga Pass to Twin Lakes   51

III.   TRANS-SIERRA SKI TOURS   55
   A. The Sierra High Route   57
   B. The Great Western Divide   63
   C. The Monarch Divide   67
   D. The Evolution Loop   71
   E. The Silver Divide   77
   F. The Yosemite Border Tour   81
   G. Yosemite Tours   87

IV.   SELECTED SHORT TOURS   91
   1. The Cottonwood Lakes Area   93
   2. The Whitney Area   97
   3. The Kearsarge Area   101
   4. The Palisades Area   105
   5. The South Lake Area   109
   6. The Lake Sabrina Area   113
   7. The North Lake Area   117
   8. The Buttermilk Area   121
   9. The Pine Creek Area   125
   10. The Rock Creek Area   129

11. The Hilton Area 133
12. The Convict Area 137
13. The Mammoth Area 141
14. The Tioga Area 147
15. The Tuolumne Area 151
16. The Green & Virginia Lakes Area 155
17. The Sawtooth Ridge Area 159
18. The Mineral King Area 163

V. CLASSIC SKI PEAKS 167

  1. Mt. Williamson 168
  2. Kearsarge Peak 169
  3. Mt. Perkins 170
  4. Birch Mountain 171
  5. Basin Mountain 172
  6. Mt. Tom 173
  7. Mt. Morgan S. 174
  8. Mt. Morgan N. 175
  9. Mt. McGee 176
10. Bloody Mountain 177
11. Mt. Ritter 178
12. Carson Peak 179
13. Mt. Wood 180
14. Mt. Gibbs 181
15. Mt. Dana 182
16. Dunderberg Peak 184
17. Matterhorn Peak 185

VI. APPENDIX 187

VII. BIBLIOGRAPHY 189

INTRODUCTION

THE HIGH SIERRA IS PERHAPS the finest range in the world to seek the challenges of backcountry skiing. The abundant snowfall, moderate weather and inviting terrain make it a perfect place to explore on skis. The blanket of snow not only makes travel easier, it also removes all sign of summer use and allows you to believe you are perhaps the first to explore an area.

However, it can be a very harsh environment. Heavy snowfalls and high avalanche danger, combined with often very remote locations, can make even the shortest backcountry ski tours very serious expeditions. As such, it is essential to have a thorough understanding and knowledge of routefinding, navigation, winter camping, basic mountaineering skills, first aid and avalanche hazard determination to safely attempt these routes.

The season for backcountry skiing in the Sierra generally runs from early November to mid-July. However, conditions generally are safest in the spring: March through June usually are the best months for these tours. Summer skiing also can be found on the high glaciers and permanent snowfields of the range.

There are many high roads and trailheads that begin to open in the spring, providing easy access to the high country. However, the only road that crosses the section of the Sierra covered in this book is the Tioga Pass road in Yosemite National Park – and this usually is closed from early November to mid-May.

I have chosen to limit this book to the "High Sierra:" a region bounded by Olancha Peak and Coyote Peaks to the south and Tower Peak to the north. This area includes all Sierra peaks over 12,000 feet, and literally thousands of square miles of wilderness. Almost all of this region is federally-protected, including all of the Yosemite, Sequoia and King's Canyon National Parks, as well as the Golden Trout, John Muir, Ansel Adams and Hoover Wilderness areas.

With such a large area to cover, it's clear that a definitive guide to all the potential ski routes in the Sierra would be a nearly impossible task. Not only that, it would take a lot of the adventure out of exploring the High Sierra on skis. Therefore, I have only included what I feel are the most spectacular and representative routes. These can be seen as backpacking trips on skis, where the primary goal is to see the country rather than seek out challenging ski descents. For folks that like the steeps, I have included some of more accessible and challenging short tours and ski peaks. And for those who just want to experience the snowy High Sierra, I have included some wonderful easy short tours and base camps.

GETTING THERE

California seems like such a worldly and accessible place, but in reality much of the state is roadless mountain wilderness. The Sierra Nevada forms a very effective barrier to travel, especially in winter, so in many cases the old saying "You can't get there from here," is almost true. As the crest of the Sierra runs more or less north to south, access generally is from the west or the east.

The one road crossing the segment of the Sierra covered in this book is the Tioga Pass road, which is closed half of the year. This fact stymies the dozens of tourists every day trying to get to Yosemite Valley from the east in the winter – these folks can be seen belatedly reading their maps more closely after reaching the locked gate just west of Lee Vining. They face driving 500 miles or more out of their way to reach a destination only 40 or so air miles from where their car sits. I use this example to show why "Trans-Sierra" tours impose much greater travel logistics than simply parking your car one side of the range or the other. Sometimes it's faster to ski across than drive around!

There are ways to reach the High Sierra – it just takes some effort. The closest airports to this region are in Fresno (for the west side) and Reno (for the east). Bus service to the mountains exists from these areas, but is very impractical for ski tours. A rental car is much more appropriate.

For people with cars, the Sierra is bounded by parallel roads: State Highway 99 on the west and U.S. Highway 395 on the east. U.S. Highway 50 and Interstate 80 reach these roads both from the Bay Area and the states to the east. U.S. Highway 6 reaches Bishop and areas south along 395 from the east, and State Highway 14 connects 395 to Los Angeles.

Spur roads heading into the range from 99 and 395 reach the trailheads. Fresno is the hub of the west side, with State Highway 198 accessing Mineral King and Giant Forest via Visalia, and State Highway 180 reaching King's Canyon and Giant Forest via Grant Grove. State Highway 168 leads east to the roadend at Huntington Lake, and State Highway 41 leads north through Oakhurst to Yosemite Valley and the spur to Badger Pass.

Bishop lies midway between Reno and Los Angeles on Highway 395 and serves as the hub for the east side and crest tours. The smaller towns of Lone Pine, Independence, Big Pine, Mammoth Lakes, June Lake, Lee Vining and Bridgeport line the route, and are host to basic supplies and amenities including grocery stores, showers and restaurants. There are numerous year-round campgrounds near most of the trailheads. Addresses and phone numbers for the U.S. Park and Forest Service offices administering these regions are found in the back of this book.

USING THIS GUIDE

The tours in this book are really backpacking trips on skis. The first section deals with skiing the Sierra Crest from Horseshoe Meadow to Twin Lakes. I've broken this into several three- to seven-day segments, but they can be added together to produce a ski equivalent of hiking the John Muir Trail. The second section deals with "Trans-Sierra" tours, which follow the natural lines created by the major east-west divides in the heart of the range. The third section deals with shorter tours and base camps near the crest. The final section covers a few of the most classic ski peaks along the east side of the range.

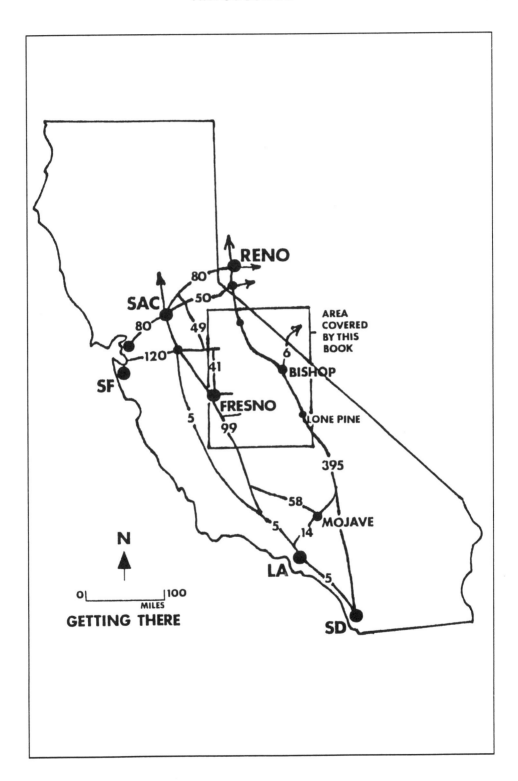

AREA
COVERED
BY THIS
BOOK

RENO

SAC

SF

BISHOP

FRESNO

LONE PINE

395

MOJAVE

LA

SD

80

80

50

49

120

41

5

99

58

5

14

5

6

N

0   100
MILES

GETTING THERE

Each route description includes the tour's difficulty level, distance, trailheads and pertinent maps. On the tour descriptions, I also list the approximate elevations of important features as a rough guide to the relative elevation gain and loss. The "John Muir Wilderness" three-map series is the best map resource for the area, as it combines most of the maps needed onto two large sheets.

I have made no distinction between "alpine" and "nordic" on these tours. Snow conditions can vary greatly, so any of these routes might be easy one year and very technical the next. I have based the classifications on "average" conditions. What you find on your tour may be entirely different.

This classification system is a modification of mountaineering's Class 1 to 5 scale and I have incorporated the equivalent alpine ski area grade into the description.

Class 1: Gentle marked trails; Green Dot "beginner" terrain.

Class 2: More difficult off-piste ; Blue Square "Intermediate" terrain.

Class 3: Steep slopes, climbing off-skis; Black Diamond "advanced" terrain.

Class 4: Technical mountaineering terrain; Double Black Diamond "expert" terrain.

Class 5: Extremely technical terrain; the realm of the "extreme" skier.

A happy camper in the Sierra.   Photo: John Moynier

Note: There are no Class 1 or Class 5 tours in this book; most are in the class 3 range and should be considered ski mountaineering. Conditions may be such that mountaineering skills as well as strong skiing skills may be required. Ice axes should be carried, and ropes, crampons and other climbing equipment may be needed for an ascent or descent.

The descriptions in this book are designed to very rough guides and only act as a companion to USGS topo maps. The actual route you take may very well be different from my description. I have left out information concerning specific route and campsite selection in the spirit of adventure and personal responsibility.

HISTORY OF SIERRA SKI TOURING

It's tempting to trace the roots of High Sierra ski touring back to Snowshoe Thompson, who carried the mail across the range on skis in the mid-1800s. However, Snowshoe and his fellow Norwegian miners primarily stuck to the Tahoe region in the north. Skiing in the High Sierra didn't really become popular until after World War I. One of the first ski areas was Rock Creek Lodge, which was constructed in the 1920s as a "Little Switzerland" resort intended to rival those in the Alps.

About this time, snow surveyors began skiing into the range to check the water stored in the snowpack. This experience provided Orland Bartholomew with the skills to ski the John Muir Trail in the winter of 1928. Orland took three months for this solo journey, coming out of the backcountry only occasionally and making use of pre-placed caches. Also at this time, men such as Otto Steiner – trained in the Alps and expert skiers – were making impressive ski descents and very fast traverses of the range.

The Sierra Club's Ski Mountaineers became active in the mid-thirties, and by 1940 David Brower and his cohorts had made winter ski ascents of Mt. Lyell, the peaks of the Palisades and many others. Norman Clyde also was a very avid skier, and spent many winters caretaking various small lodges along the east side. Springtime usually found Norman and his fellow Ski Mountaineers setting up a base camp somewhere near the crest, making many peak ascents and descents on skis and generally having themselves a blast. The lasting legacy of this group was the landmark Manual of Ski Mountaineering, written by Brower and published by the Sierra Club. The group also published articles in the Sierra Club Bulletin, as well as in Touring Topics and Westways magazines.

The range continued to be explored on skis by California Snow Survey and Department of Water and Power (DWP) hydrographers including Dave McCoy, owner of Mammoth Mountain Ski Area. Dave and his friends formed the Eastern Sierra Ski Club. In addition to making difficult descents of peaks in the eastern Sierra, they carted around a portable rope tow to most east side roadheads, including Whitney Portal, Onion Valley, Glacier Lodge and Mt. Mc Gee.

Other eastside ski clubs also operated lifts in what are now prime backcountry ski locations, including the Whitewing, Carson Peak, Lee Vining Canyon and Conway summit areas. In fact, there used to be a downhill race from the summit of Carson Peak to the base, with winning times often between five and ten minutes! Many of these ski pioneers, like Hans Georg, Ed Heath and Wally McPherson, served as part of the ski troops during World War II.

Since that war, there has been continued growth in backcountry skiing. Dave McCoy's kids were part of the next generation of ski explorers, as Carl "Peanut" McCoy, along with Doug Robinson, became the second known party to ski the Muir Trail in 1970. They used randonnee gear and skied the route in one continuous push.

A guidebook to ski descents in the Sierra was published in 1971. This book, *Sierra Spring Ski-Touring*, was written by H.J. Burhenne with Norm Wilson, and served as an inspiration for this next generation. Nordic skiing became popular, with David and Susan Beck touring the Sierra High Route in 1975 and the Muir Trail in 1976 using lightweight Nordic gear. David later wrote his own backcountry guidebook called *Ski Touring in California*, which last was published in 1980.

Touring below Mt. Abbot.   Photo: John Moynier

In the seventies and eighties, many of the most active backcountry skiers came from the Yosemite climbing community. These climbers were tired of the pressure for first ascents on the rocks and resolved to keep first ski descents unpublished and couloirs unnamed.

Tom Carter, Allan Bard and Chris Cox, in particular, sought ever higher lines along the crests of the divides. The culmination of their efforts was the "Redline" tour, which follows the political boundary (the red line on the map) along the very crest of the Sierra. This tour involved linking many challenging descents off the highest peaks, and is the highest skiable expression of the Crest Tour.

Speed traverses of the High Sierra have been popular since Otto Steiner's days. Many of the tours in this book have been done in under 24 hours by very fit individuals, including the High Route (by Doug Robinson in 1984). Skiing the entire Crest Route continuously generally takes about a month – or longer, if there are storms. However, in the early eighties a pair of Colorado Outward Bound instructors waited all winter for perfect conditions, then sprinted the route in seven days, taking only the barest minimum of gear!

For the most part, I've tried to keep to the philosophy of "Everytime's the first" by not publishing accounts of first descents. I'll make an exception, however, in the case of Chris Landry. Chris's definition of the sport of "extreme" skiing was: "If you fall, you die." He tested these limits by skiing the Mendel Couloir, a very challenging alpine ice climb, in 1981. This feat has not, to my knowledge, been surpassed in the decade since.

However, Dave McCoy's grandson Davey McCoy, and his extreme skiing friends like Scot Schmidt and Glen Plake, are just now beginning to apply the type of ski mountaineering found on the great peaks of the Alps to the cliffs and couloirs of the Sierra crest. Who knows what will be next – the East Face of Whitney, perhaps?

WINTER AWARENESS

HIGH SIERRA WEATHER

Weather in the High Sierra, as in any major mountain range, often is unpredictable. Winters here generally are typified by long periods of wonderfully clear weather interspersed with intense storms that can last a week or more. These patterns primarily are dictated by the winter jet stream and the location of the Great Basin high pressure center. Normal winter daytime temperatures at 10,000 feet are in the teens or low twenties, with nighttime lows near or just below zero (Fahrenheit). Springtime is warmer, with highs in the forties and lows in the teens or low twenties.

Winter storms generally come from the southwest, bringing warm, moisture-laden air in from the Pacific. These storms often bring new snowfalls of two to three feet, and dumps of six feet or more are not uncommon. They also usually are accompanied by strong winds out of the southwest, which heavily load north- to east-facing slopes. It is rare for cold northern storms to reach this far south, but when they do, bitter cold temperatures arrive and may linger for a week or more.

Occasionally, the Pacific storm tract sets its sights on the High Sierra, and storms will stack up out to Japan. This weather pattern can set up for entire winters, as it did in 1969, 1978 and 1983, when over 50 feet of snow fell during the season, or can set up for a shorter time, as in February 1986, when 20 feet of snow fell in one week! These major Pacific systems often result from the collision of cold air masses from the gulf of Alaska with warm, moist air from near Hawaii. The midwinter jet stream funnels these mega-storms right at us, forming what's affectionately known as the "Pineapple Express." When these conditions are forecasted, it's best to postpone your touring plans and enjoy the fine deep-snow skiing at the lift-served areas.

A unique aspect of Sierra winter storms is that after they pass, the winds shift, blowing cold and dry out of the north or east. These "Nevada Lows" often have a scouring effect, loading snow on the "wrong" side of a ridge and destroying the powder skiing. These winds also often pack the snow into a Styrofoam-like surface that offers "primo" windpacked skiing. Under these circumstances, however, a ground blizzard can be especially nasty, and you really have to protect against frostbite .

A TYPICAL WINTER

Generally, winters begin with a couple of decent snowfalls in late September or October. These early storms can be very cold, and may last a week or more. Thanksgiving traditionally is the beginning of the ski season and often is a stormy time, as is Christmas break. The best powder skiing often comes before the New Year. However, if there is not a good early base, the entire winter's snowpack will be underlain by an unstable layer of depth hoar.

After the New Year, there always seems to be a period when a high pressure system settles over the region, and we get a couple of weeks of cold, clear weather. This can be a great time to head into the backcountry, provided you don't mind long, cold nights and short, chilly days.

February, March and early April traditionally are the periods of heaviest snowfall. Long tours in these months must be planned with an eye for long-term weather forecasts, or you might find yourself pinned down by one of those major Pacific storm systems. Because of this possibility, most folks plan long tours for later in spring, when the weather is more stable and the snowpack has settled.

In spring, freezing temperatures at night and warm temperatures during the day work to create the "corn" snow for which the Sierra is justly famous. This mature melt-freeze snow resembles glacial neve, and provides an ideal surface for skiing. However, if day-time temperatures are high and night-time temperatures fail to drop below zero, you might be in for some tough sledding, and climax avalanches may carry away the entire snowpack down to the ground.

We really are fortunate to enjoy such a long ski season in the Sierra. About the time folks in Colorado or Utah are hanging up their skis and hopping on their mountain bikes, the skiing here is just starting to get good. Mammoth Mountain Ski Area often has been open for skiing through the Fourth of July, and in many years, the backcountry has stayed good throughout the summer! That's why a lot of us never put our skis away for the season – there always are a few turns to be had on the small glaciers and permanent snowfields hidden along the crest.

Avalanches

Many Sierra backcountry skiers choose to believe there is no such thing as avalanche hazard, refusing to let any negative thoughts intrude on their ski fun. Extensive experience in more hazardous areas has left other folks blind to the dangers of avalanches in the Sierra Nevada. And there are others who are just ignorant of the dangers of avalanches.

Photo: John Moynier

Many of the tours in this book are threatened by avalanches.

No matter the mindset, the plain truth is that the Sierra does have avalanches – very real and destructive ones – and anyone heading out on these tours must recognize the risks involved. In all seriousness, avalanche risk should be first and foremost in everyone's thoughts. In fact, each and every one of these tours involves terrain that may develop avalanche hazard. This doesn't mean you definitely will be at risk, but you must have a strong enough background in evaluating snow conditions to assess when and if there is an avalanche hazard in order to enjoy the slopes safely.

It is not my intention to list every potential avalanche slope or hazardous area on each of these tours. In fact, I have mentioned only the most obvious and frequent avalanche performers that may be encountered. It is the responsibility of each member on a tour to evaluate their own risk when travelling through this terrain.

Avalanche hazard awareness is developed through education and experience. There are many opportunities to receive hands-on field training in avalanche awareness. Anyone attempting these tours should have taken an avalanche course with practical field work in evaluation and rescue techniques. Without this knowledge, you are playing "avalanche roulette" every time you head into the backcountry.

BASIC AVALANCHE HAZARD AWARENESS

Most backcountry skiers eventually will find themselves exposed to some avalanche hazard. In fact, most of the slopes we enjoy skiing can be classified as prime avalanche terrain. In a sense, ignorance is bliss: As we learn more about the conditions that lead to instability, we can recall instances when we were more at risk than we realized.

The key to skiing the backcountry safely then, is learning how to recognize hazardous conditions, relating this information to the route we've chosen and understanding how conditions may change with time. Judgement, knowledge and experience become our guides. We listen to the snow, feel it with our poles and skis and constantly evaluate each step or turn.

It's important to note that weather events are the key to determining immediate and future hazard. Most slides occur within 48 hours of a storm or wind-loading event. New deposition of an inch an hour or 12 inches total should be warning signs. Even moderate winds can increase the hazard, depositing dangerous slabs on leeward slopes. Temperatures well above or below freezing can lead to decreased stability of the snowpack, as can rain or warm wind. Local ski areas, shops or government agencies can give you this information.

The snowpack itself also is of primary interest. Layers of snow within the pack can act cohesively as slabs. Poor bonding between these layers can lead to weaknesses in the strength of the pack. This is especially true of buried ice crusts or thin layers of surface hoar.

The processes that lead to increased or decreased stability also are important. A deep snowpack and moderate temperatures will result in a small temperature gradient through the pack from ground to surface. The physics of this situation leads to greater snowpack stability through equi-temperature or "ET" processes, which result in a net decrease in snow crystal size and a net increase in the bonding strength between the crystals.

Skiing into avalanche terrain.

Photo: John Moynier

Shallow snowpacks and/or very cold temperatures lead to a steep temperature gradient between the ground and the surface. The resultant "TG" processes "rot" the snow from the ground or a buried layer up towards the surface by destroying the bonds between the crystals as the crystals themselves grow.

Alternating warm days and cold nights will lead to a very strong snowpack, bonded by the melt-freeze or "MF" process. Free water in the snowpack re-freezes to glue the crystals together.

All of these processes might occur in the same snowpack. You can check snowpack conditions by digging a pit in the snow or probing with your ski pole. If you are unsure about a slope, you should perform a shovel shear or Rutschblock ski test to determine stability. Before you leave on your trip, check the local avalanche forecast for information regarding the snowpack.

When planning a route, remember that slope angles of 25 to 45 degrees (advanced to expert alpine ski runs) are the most likely to slide, especially on convex slopes that are under more internal tension. These are the slopes I call "steep" in this book. Steeper slopes generally slough off accumulations, but wet snow can stick to very steep slopes. Cornices often build up on the ridge tops and threaten more moderate slopes below. When skiing along a ridge, always stay much further back from the edge than appears necessary, as cornices can be weak bridges over gaps in the crest.

Once in the backcountry, it's important to pick a route that avoids primary avalanche terrain if at all possible, as conditions may change from day to day or hour to hour. When in doubt, pick a route that follows a ridge top or wide valley bottom, if possible. Look for signs of previous avalanche activity, such as obvious slide paths, damaged trees or other vegetation, and debris cones – and avoid them. Signs of recent avalanches (such as fracture crowns and blocks of debris) on slopes of a similar aspect to the one you want to ski, as well as slope angle, are very important clues to the hazardous nature of your route. Trees generally are safer than open slopes, but they don't guarantee safety.

If you must travel in a hazardous area, limit your exposure. Cross one at a time, with avalanche beacons on "Transmit" and all eyes on the person crossing. Take advantage of safer areas like dense timber, rock outcrops, ridges and wide valley bottoms. If you must ascend or descend a dangerous slope, stay close to the edge and chose as vertical a line as possible. Kicking steps straight up or down is much safer than cutting the slope with traverses, turns or sitzmarks. Don't assume a slope is safe just because someone else has skied it, and remember that activity on a lower-angled slope can trigger steeper slopes above, or sympathetically release a slope some distance away.

Finally, the best overall strategy is to use caution and be prepared. Make sure everyone has a functioning avalanche transceiver and knows how to use it. These should be turned to "Transmit" at the start of the day, checked, and left on until safe in camp. Each person also should carry a sturdy shovel and avalanche probe poles.

Always make sure everyone understands and approves of the group's objectives and that alternate routes have been taken into account. Listen to your intuition. If your gut tells you things are amiss, the time to act is now. Don't let the idea that "I don't want to spoil it for the group" lead to tragedy. Stand up for your opinion and don't worry about being a "party pooper." It is much better to err on the safe side and come back another day than to have to dig a buddy out of a pile of debris. The ski area maxim: "Be aware, ski with care," is the absolute law of the backcountry. Backcountry skiing can be a very safe and rewarding experience if everyone accepts these responsibilities.

WINTER TRAVEL

Safe travel in the wintry Sierra depends on a number of skills. The most obvious are skiing skills, but they are not really the most important. In fact, just being solid on kick turns and traverses is much more important than being able to do jump telemarks or parallel squiggles in powder. The middle of a long tour is no place to practice your tele turns with a heavy pack on. Balancing under the weight of the pack while sliding on these skinny little sticks is plenty challenging enough.

When in doubt, leave your climbing skins on for the descents, as well as ascents. It's certainly easier to slowly glide down from a pass on skins than to wildly step turn through rocks or pick yourself and pack up over and over again. Remember, there is no ski patrol out here – you must be entirely self-sufficient and capable of effecting any self-rescue necessary.

More important than being a good skier is the ability to find routes and orienteer. You absolutely must be able to read a map and know how to use a compass both to orient the map and find your way in a blizzard or white-out. The snowy Sierra can be a very disorienting place, and many very experienced mountaineers have gotten very lost and very embarrassed on these very tours because they didn't read the maps very well (Yea, verily though I say . . .).

Learning to navigate by landmarks comes with practice, but picking the easiest route through cliffs or a forest, or other tricky terrain takes much more experience. I don't presume that I know better than you which specific pass or route to take on these tours, or even which side of a lake or creek to ski on. Conditions constantly change, and a shift in the wind could put an impassible cornice over what otherwise would be a relatively easy pass. Therefore, you're on your own when it comes to the exact route you take while attempting these tours.

Along with orienteering comes avalanche hazard awareness (which is discussed elsewhere) and basic mountaineering skills such as using a rope or an ice axe. Many of the passes on these tours are steep enough that most people will feel more comfortable using an ice axe for a self-belay than their skis or poles. For firm windboard or icy conditions, crampons may even be needed, or time-consuming steps must be cut.

Due to the exposure of some of these passes over cliffs and such, some folks may want a hand line or even a belay, and it's quite possible you may even need to rappel off of a cornice or short stretch of cliff. Skiers touring in low-snow years may encounter much more off-ski climbing than in heavier snow years, but cornices may make the bigger years just as challenging.

The same care and caution should be used travelling over the loose rock found in some of these areas, as well as with creek and lake crossings. It always is worth looking for a solid snow bridge before attempting to cross a stream, especially if you can see or hear running water. As far as trusting lake ice, you must use your own judgement. The ice generally is weakest at the

Skiing up toward Echo Col.   Photo: John Moynier

inlet and outlet, but there often are hidden thin spots – or even open water – in the middle of larger lakes. There have been a number of cases of backcountry skiers breaking through the ice of lakes and drowning because their pack and skis weighed them down.

As long as I'm preaching caution and self-sufficiency, let me add that it is very important that everyone in the party have a basic understanding of mountaineering first aid and know how to recognize and treat the most common problems like blisters, frostbite, hypothermia and altitude sickness. Someone in the party should have enough experience to recognize the symptoms of edema and the group's first aid kit should be able to handle anything from bad sunburn to snow blindness to a broken femur. This versatility should also apply to equipment repairs in the field and transporting an injured member of your party by making an emergency sled.

SNOW CAMPING

I mentioned that most of these tours were like backpacking on snow. However, that "on snow" part does lead to some major differences. While camping under a tree in the summer might be romantic, in winter, it can be deadly. Heavily-weighted branches and snow bombs can drop at any time. Beware of exposed campsites at the foot of a pass or ridge, which might be in a runout zone for rockfall, avalanches or cornice releases. Flat meadows may make inviting sites, yet they're notorious traps for cold air.

Often a water source is of prime importance for a camp. You generally can break through the ice of a lake or stream with a shovel to get water, rather than melting snow, but you'll have to treat it just like you would in summer. Camps with flat rocks or sand allow you to stay drier and spread yourselves and gear out to dry – it's especially important to dry out your sleeping bag.

You'll need to pack down a tent platform with your skis or feet. Building shallow walls around the tent will help you keep from having to hold the tent down in a storm. If you are making a base camp, it's worth the effort to dig out a separate kitchen, with a tarp overhead and carved-out benches to sit on.

At a base camp, it's especially important to rig some kind of latrine so you don't just deposit waste in the snow. Using "rocket boxes" or plastic buckets lined with plastic trash bags is the most environmentally-sound way to handle waste. While on the trail, you should find either a boulder field or an area that is completely and obviously far away from any water source or use area. A misplaced dump will melt through, TP and all, to water or ground below. Think where you would go in the summer, and if you can find dry ground in which to bury it, do it.

There are some other important strategies to placing winter camps. Remember, cold winds blow down canyon at night and early light in the morning is more important than late light in the evening. Placing a camp in the morning shadow of a big peak definitely will make it hard to get out of your bag and into frozen boots early in the day.

Camp according to your situation – you may want to plan the camps so if a storm comes in, you won't be trapped on the wrong side of a pass or in a hazardous location; or you might want to place yourself so you can get over a pass early in the morning while the avalanche hazard is lower – or later in the day when an icy surface has softened up.

Descending from Mount Emerson/Piute Crags.   Photo: John Moynier

EQUIPMENT

I don't think much needs to be said about ski equipment. All of these tours and descents have been done with modern cross-country gear: high-topped, leather boots with stiff soles, metal-edged, single-cambered telemark skis and avalanche probe poles. However, randonnee equipment also works fine, especially for those who want more downhill control. Alpine ski gear is quite appropriate for "hike up and ski down"-style peak descents, as are snowboards, zippy sleds . . . and even little metal saucers for that matter.

For all of these, just make sure your boots fit well and are comfortable before you start trudging in them, because walking or skinning up a hill is very different than downhill skiing at a lift-served area. Bad blisters will ruin even the most spectacular tour.

Climbing skins are worth their weight in gold. In the Sierra, adhesive-backed, nylon skins are more popular than strap-on styles because they allow you to edge on hard snow. Synthetic skins provide decent glide while maintaining maximum uphill grip, and dry out quickly. It's a good idea to touch up the glue before every trip, but duct tape can help if glue starts to fail on the tour.

Internal frame packs are the best bet for the longer tours, as they keep your center of gravity close to your body for better balance. A warm sleeping bag and pad are essential, as is some form of shelter. Four-season free-standing tents are the most popular, although many folks prefer the "pyramid"-style tarps because of the versatility and weight savings.

A good, hot-burning stove that is maintenance-free is most important – the hotter it is, the faster it will melt snow for water. Taking food that you like is as important as its weight and ease of preparation. You burn a lot of calories just staying warm in winter. Anyone for a second helping of tasteless gruel?

Other specific equipment for backcountry touring should include a light ice axe. If for no other reason, it can stake your tent down while you're out skiing. Most folks take along a 100 foot or longer coil of 7mm rope on more difficult tours for the reasons stated previously. Everyone in the group should have a functioning avalanche transceiver and a sturdy shovel and know how to use them. There should be a least one good first aid kit and repair kit in the group. The repair kit should include a light pair of vice-grips, duct tape, pole-splinting materials, spare baskets, 5-minute epoxy and binding repair equipment, as well as a means of making a sled out of skis, shovels and poles.

Other obvious "essential" equipment should include extra water bottles, toilet paper, a headlamp, spare lighters or matches, map and compass, knife, and really good sunglasses and sunscreen. You also may want to bring an altimeter.

CLOTHING

There are so many good, synthetic alternatives to down, wool and cotton these days that I don't need to mention them. By now everyone's probably sick of the "layering" concept, too. However, choosing what to bring and wear is important. You'll want to wear just enough to stay warm during the day's trek, but not so much that you'll overheat while slogging over a pass, and you must have enough warm stuff with you to enjoy the evening light after dinner.

A good warm hat as well as a sun hat both are very important. Weather-proofed pants and jacket make stormy days a lot nicer, as do a good pair of gloves or mittens and a neck gaiter or scarf. Bicycling gloves are very comfortable on sunny spring tours. Extra dry socks and a pair of camp booties are a necessity. I feel the same way about keeping a warm, dry set of clothes to sleep in – you'll really be a lot more comfortable. However, you must remember that you have to carry all these clothes and you'll have to fit them all into your comfortably-sleek touring pack.

WINTER ECOLOGY

GEOGRAPHY

The name Sierra Nevada literally means "a great, snowy range." The mountains are California's topographic backbone, and run basically northwest to southeast for almost 400 miles along the eastern edge of the state, from Mt. Lassen to the Garlock vault in the Mojave Desert. The range generally is 40 to 80 miles wide and constitutes the largest continuous range in the lower 48 states.

The region from Cirque Peak to Tower Peak is considered the "High Sierra." Here, 11 peaks rise over 14,000 feet and hundreds more top 12,000 and 13,000 feet. Even the lowest passes in this area are over 9,000 feet high. Extensive vertical movement on the Sierra Nevada fault in this region has produced an almost unbroken wall dropping up to 10,000 vertical feet from the crest to the valleys to the east.

Heading west from the crest are numerous, prominent divides. These separate the major rivers of the Sierra, which all drain to the west. These rivers are, from south to north: the Kern, Kaweah, Kings, San Joaquin, Merced and Tuolumne. Many of these rivers follow very deep canyons, reaching depths of 6,000 feet or more. As a result, the tours in this book mainly follow the crest or the tops of these divides, and generally stay above timberline for much of their length.

The major geologic factors that produced the Sierra Nevada as it is seen today were uplifting along faults and erosion by rivers and glaciation (all of which is still going on). The major periods of North American glaciation carved out the classic U-shaped canyons so typical of the Sierra. Particularly spectacular in this regard are the Muro Blanco, Le Conte and Bubbs Creek canyons on the Kings, the Kern River Canyon and of course, Tenaya canyon and the Yosemite Valley. The wonderful domes of the Tuolumne area also were shaped and polished by glaciers. At the mouths of the major eastside canyons, glaciation has deposited massive moraines extending out into the high desert.

GEOLOGY

Much of the geology of this region of the Sierra Nevada will be hidden by snow on these tours . . . and it's pretty monotonous, anyway. For the most part, the rocks in this part of the Sierra are granite, part of the great Sierra batholith. In a few areas, the older sedimentary and metamorphic cap rocks are still present. These are called "roof pendants," with the oldest being in the Convict Lake area. Here, 500-million-year-old limestones, shales and dolomites form a very colorful contrast to the more common grey and orange granites. These rocks also have been greatly folded, so that entire mountainsides display fantastic twisted shapes and patterns.

There also are metamorphosed volcanics present, especially in the Mineral King area and the Ritter Range. The spectacularly jagged Minarets are remnants of the fractured core of an ancient volcano. Scattered volcanic cones, like Mammoth Mountain, line the eastern Sierra, with the youngest cones, found in the June Lake area, less than 500 years old.

BOTANY

Again, most of the plants will be buried by snow, but it's worth noting the presence of certain trees, the most unique of which are the giant sequoias. There is a broad belt of these magnificent trees along the western side of the range, and ski touring through areas like Giant Forest is truly a humbling experience. Since most of these tours are near timberline, you'll see mostly lodgepole and whitebark pines, with scattered stands of red fir, hemlock and aspen. Sierra junipers form stately sentinels in the north, and foxtail pines, curiously, are found on the high benches west of Mt. Whitney. Tours in the eastern Sierra, especially in the Mammoth area, also meander among the wonderfully fragrant Jeffrey pine.

CRITTERS

Many of the animals of the Sierra hide in the winter. They either head down to lower elevations to escape the harshness of winter, like deer, or sleep away the snows, like the black bear. The two large animals you're most likely to see are the Sierra hare, which takes on a white winter coat, and its companion, the mountain coyote. It's not uncommon to follow coyote tracks over the passes on these tours, or even to the summit of a snowy peak! It's also a real treat to be serenaded at night by a group of happy coyotes or be followed along at a distance while you're skiing.

If you're lucky, you may spot a band of bighorn sheep in some of the eastside areas, or a mountain lion returning to a cached deer carcass. Black bears can be a problem in the spring, as they're quite hungry and used to stealing backpackers' food. Likewise, the fat furballs known as marmots also can be a nuisance at a spring base camps, emerging from their mazes of tunnels to chew on unattended boots and packs.

Aside from these creatures, you're most likely to be harassed by the mountain chickadee, landing on your pack or ski pole looking for handouts, or the stealthy meadow vole, which can be quite persistent about getting into food caches. Louder, yet less brave, are the Clark's nutcracker and the chickaree, a squirrel that provides the main food source for the shy pine martin.

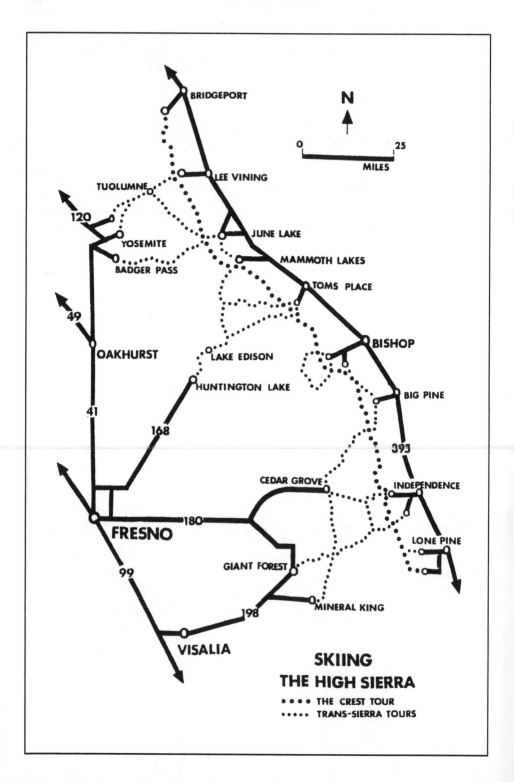

N

0 |—————————| 25
MILES

BRIDGEPORT

LEE VINING

TUOLUMNE

120

JUNE LAKE

YOSEMITE

MAMMOTH LAKES

BADGER PASS

TOMS PLACE

49

BISHOP

OAKHURST

LAKE EDISON

HUNTINGTON LAKE

BIG PINE

41

168

395

CEDAR GROVE

INDEPENDENCE

FRESNO

180

LONE PINE

99

GIANT FOREST

VISALIA

198

MINERAL KING

**SKIING
THE HIGH SIERRA**

● ● ● ● THE CREST TOUR
· · · · · TRANS-SIERRA TOURS

SIERRA CREST TOURS

SKIING THE SIERRA CREST is quite an adventure. It's been called a "low-level flight over some of the most spectacular country on earth." The Crest Route follows a much higher line than the John Muir Trail, yet takes perhaps an even more skiable route. I have broken the whole route into seven segments, each of which is a three- to seven-day tour in itself. These segments begin at Horseshoe Meadows, which is south of Mt. Whitney, and end at Twin Lakes near Bridgeport.

Obviously, you can ski either from south to north or north to south. For consistency, I have described them all from south to north (I personally like skiing away from the sun). The direction you chose, however, probably will be based on ski conditions. Early in the year it's often better to head south; this way you climb up the transitional snow and ski down the south-facing corn snow. Later in the year, the south slopes might be more patchy and heading north gives you finer downhill runs.

All of these crest tours are reached from the east, but obviously you can combine segments of Trans-Sierra and crest tours for a super loop trip. You also will have to do some form of car shuttle for all of these or try some epic hitch-hike, bike and hike combination to get back to your car. As with the rest of this book, the elevations I have included are approximate and are only included to provide an idea of the relative gain and loss in elevation.

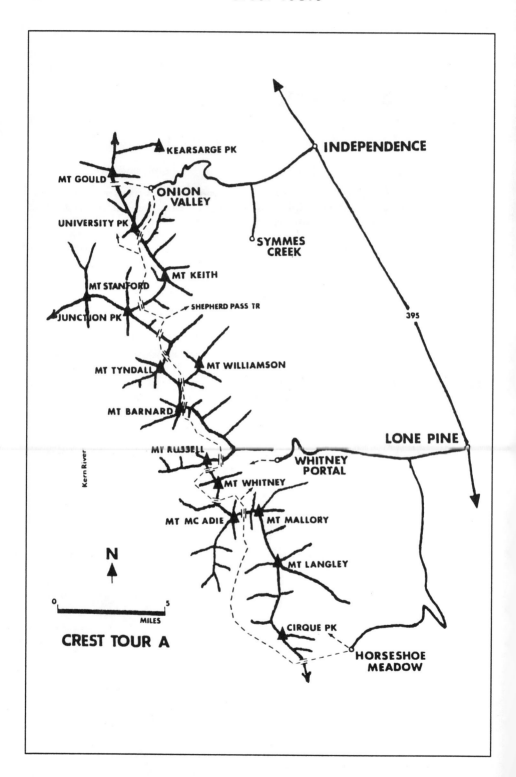

KEARSARGE PK

MT GOULD

ONION VALLEY

UNIVERSITY PK

MT KEITH

MT STANFORD

SHEPHERD PASS TR

JUNCTION PK

MT TYNDALL

MT WILLIAMSON

MT BARNARD

Kern River

MT RUSSELL

MT WHITNEY

WHITNEY PORTAL

MT MC ADIE

MT MALLORY

MT LANGLEY

N

0   5
MILES

CIRQUE PK

CREST TOUR A

INDEPENDENCE

SYMMES CREEK

395

LONE PINE

HORSESHOE MEADOW

A. HORSESHOE MEADOW TO ONION VALLEY

Difficulty: Class 3-4
Distance: Approx. 48 miles
Trailheads: Horseshoe Meadow and Onion Valley
Maps: Mt. Whitney, Olancha 15-minute or
Cirque Peak, Johnson Peak, Mt. Langley, Mt. Whitney, Mt. Williamson,
Kearsarge Peak 7.5 minute

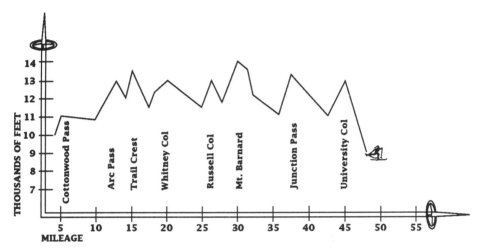

The Whitney area is a land of contrasts: very sheer east faces of peaks and much gentler western slopes; high, unglaciated plateaus and very large glacial cirques and canyons. This area also has some of the highest lakes in the Sierra and provides very skiable (at very high altitude) touring potential. This section allows you to ease into the backcountry with the gentle crossing of Cottonwood Pass before tackling the very high and rugged country around Mt. Whitney, the highest peak in the lower 48 states. This segment also can be broken in two by using Whitney Portal as an entry/exit point.

DESCRIPTION

From Lone Pine, take the Whitney Portal Road west, then turn onto the Horseshoe Meadow Road and follow the switchbacks up the escarpment to the road end.

From Horseshoe Meadow (9,600 ft.) climb gradually up to Cottonwood Pass (11,150 ft.) and connect with the Pacific Crest Trail, which circles past Chicken Spring Lake through sparse forests to the Rock Creek drainage. Take the Siberia Pass Trail north from the junction with the PCT (11,100 ft.), and follow it up Rock Creek, passing the great cirques of Joe Devel Peak and Mt. Pickering before reaching the stunning Sky Blue Lake (11,550 ft.) and the spectacular Miter.

From the lake, follow the drainage to the northeast, skirting the south ridge of Mt. McAdie as you labor to reach Arc Pass (12,900 ft.). Here, you'll find great views of the east face of Mt. Whitney, as well as to the south, over the jagged pinnacles of Mt. Corcoran, to Mt. Langley. This great descent leads

Looking back at Mount Whitney over Russell Col.   Photo: Vern Clevenger

down to Consultation Lake (11,700 ft.) where a short climb from Lone Pine
Creek takes you around to Trail Camp (12,000 ft.). If you are ending the
segment here, follow the south fork of Lone Pine Creek down past Mirror Lake
(10,750 ft.) and out to Whitney Portal (8,400 ft.).

If you continue from Trail Camp, ski up the steep slope that harbors
Whitney's infamous switchbacks to Trail Crest (13,600 ft.) and Sequoia

Camping in Wright Lakes Basin.   Photo: Claude Fiddler

Shepherd and Junction Passes viewed from Mt. Tyndall.   Photo: Claude Fiddler

National Park. The summit of Whitney (14,495 ft.) is 2.5 miles to the north, following the summer trail. The tour over Arc Pass into Lone Pine Creek can be avoided by skiing north from Sky Blue Lake over Crabtree Pass (12,550 ft.) and up the slopes directly to Discovery Pinnacle (13,750 ft.) and down to Trail Crest.

From Trail Crest, the route heads down the west slopes of Mt. Whitney towards Guitar Lake (11,500 ft.) before circling as high as possible around the west side of Whitney to Arctic Lake (12,200 ft.). From the lake, begin climbing east to the Whitney-Russell col (13,050 ft.), which is very steep on the east side and drops you down to Iceberg Lake (12,600 ft.), below the great east face of Whitney. A fine descent below the Pinnacle Ridge leads around to Upper Boy Scout Lake (11,350 ft.), at the foot of Mt. Russell.

From the lake, a steep gully leads up to the broad saddle of the Russell-Carillion Col (13,250 ft.). This pass is very steep on its north side, dropping you quickly down past Tulainyo Lake (12,800 ft.), one of the highest lakes in the Sierra,. The descent continues to Wallace Lake (11,450 ft.) at the foot of the great mass of Mt. Barnard. The best route from here is to grunt up the southwest slopes almost to the summit (13,990 ft.) before crossing the east ridge. This is the highest point on the whole tour.

Follow the contour along the east slopes of Mt. Barnard towards the pass (13,600 ft.) just west of the summit of Trojan Peak (13,950 ft.), then drop to Lake Helen of Troy (12,500 ft.). This fine descent continues into the spectacular Williamson Bowl (12,200 ft.), which lies between the sheer east face of Mt. Tyndall and rugged Mt. Williamson. From here, a short traverse brings you to the low saddle of Shepherd Pass (12,000 ft.).

Caltech Peak seen from Tawny Point.   Photo: Vern Clevenger

The top of the pass is quite steep and avalanche-prone, but the angle soon eases as the route follows the original Muir Trail down to the bench (11,200 ft.) above The Pothole. The desert of the Owens Valley is framed by the narrow walls of Shepherd Creek below. The route heads west toward the imposing pyramid of Junction Peak before climbing steeply north to Junction Pass (13,200 ft.).

From the pass, follow the ridge north into Kings Canyon National Park before dropping down to the lake (12,100 ft.) below. A delightful run down Center Basin eventually brings you to Golden Bear Lake (11,150 ft.) below the pyramid of Center Peak. After crossing the basin, a steep climb brings you to University Pass (12,650 ft.) on the southeast shoulder of University Peak. Looking back, (give compass direction) the sheer northern wall of the Kings-Kern Divide provides a spectacular backdrop as you prepare for the great descent down the canyon past Robinson Lake (10,500 ft.) and all the way out to Onion Valley (9,200 ft.).

Carving turns below Bear Creek Spire.

Photo: John Moynier

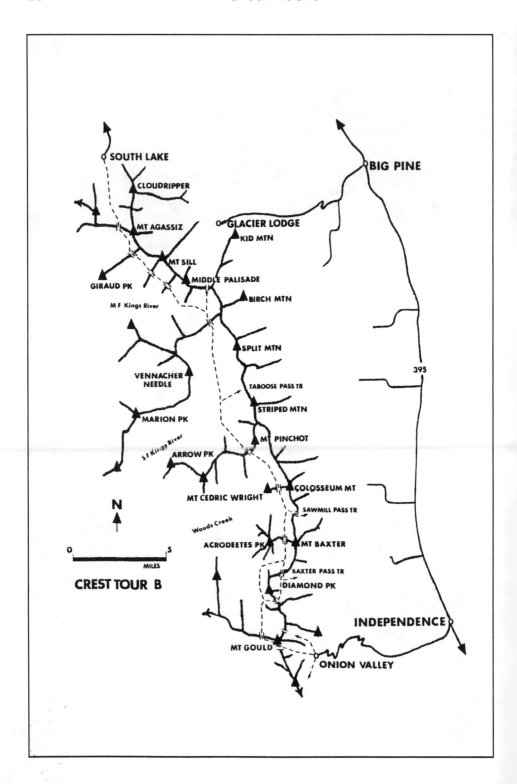

SOUTH LAKE

CLOUDRIPPER

MT AGASSIZ

MT SILL

GIRAUD PK

MIDDLE PALISADE

M F Kings River

BIG PINE

GLACIER LODGE

KID MTN

BIRCH MTN

SPLIT MTN

395

VENNACHER NEEDLE

TABOOSE PASS TR

STRIPED MTN

MARION PK

MT PINCHOT

S F Kings River

ARROW PK

N

MT CEDRIC WRIGHT

COLOSSEUM MT

SAWMILL PASS TR

0   5

MILES

CREST TOUR B

Woods Creek

ACRODEETES PK

MT BAXTER

BAXTER PASS TR

DIAMOND PK

INDEPENDENCE

MT GOULD

ONION VALLEY

B. ONION VALLEY TO SOUTH LAKE

Difficulty: Class 3-4
Distance: Approx. 55 miles
Trailheads: Onion Valley and South Lake
**Maps: Mt. Whitney, Mt. Pinchot, Big Pine, Mt. Goddard 15 minute or
Kearsarge Peak, Mt. Clarence King, Mt. Pinchot, Split Mtn., North
Palisade, Mt. Thompson 7.5 minute**

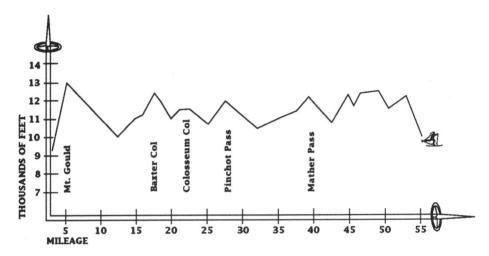

This route primarily follows the John Muir Trail, with the exception of two detours that keep the line higher along the crest, avoiding the disappointing drops down to the low elevations of Woods and Palisades Creeks. This line also follows the amazing "gunsight" route found from Baxter Lakes to Mt. Perkins. Along the way, it travels through the beautiful Rae Lakes, Palisades and Dusy Basins before heading out over Bishop Pass. The ski across the west side of the Palisades may be the most spectacular section of the entire crest.

DESCRIPTION

The route leaves Onion Valley (9,200 ft.) and follows the summer trail up to Kearsarge Pass (11,800 ft.), then climbs northwest over the shoulder of Mt. Gould (13,000 ft.) towards Mt. Rixford and Kings Canyon National Park. A steep drop from the obvious col (12,450 ft.) brings you to the trio of lakes (11,800 ft.) west of Dragon Peak, then on down to Dragon Lake (11,100 ft.). An alternate route heads up to Golden Trout Lake from Onion Valley, then over the steep Gould Pass (12,800 ft.) just north of the summit and down to these lakes.

From Dragon Lake, the route drops into the gorgeous basin of the Rae Lakes (10,550 ft.). Continue the gentle descent until you are near Dollar Lake (10,250 ft.) where the route to Baxter Pass trail is taken around the west slope of Diamond Peak and up to the largest Baxter Lake (11,150 ft.). Great views of Mt. Clarence King and Mt. Cotter to the west accompany your ascent.

Views of the headwaters of Woods Creek from Colosseum Mtn.　　　Photo: Vern Clevenger

Looking north from Pinchot Pass.　　　Photo: Claude Fiddler

Split Mountain as seen from near Middle Palisade.   Photo: Vern Clevenger

An alternate route goes around the west slopes of Black Mountain into the shallow cirque to the east. At its head, a steep col (12,250 ft.) takes you down into the Oak Creek drainage (11,500 ft.) before climbing over Baxter Pass (12,300 ft.) and dropping down to Baxter Lakes.

Once at Baxter Lakes, the route lines up for the "gunsights:" two similar passes that lie in a direct line with each other. The first climb heads up the steep slope to Baxter Col (12,500 ft.) between Mt. Baxter and Acrodeetes Peak. After a steep drop to Stocking Lake (11,400 ft.), follow the headwaters of Woods Creek down to Woods Lake (10,750 ft.), where an alternate trail heads out over Sawmill Pass to the Owens Valley.

From Woods Lake, the route heads north and climbs up to the col just east of Mt. Cedric Wright (11,600 ft.). After a short drop, follow the drainage down to Twin Lakes (10,600 ft.). The route then heads north below Mt. Perkins and joins the Muir Trail as it climbs up to Pinchot Pass (12,100 ft.), just south of Mt. Wynne. A great descent from the pass brings you past Lake Marjory (11,150 ft.) and down to the crossing of the South Fork of the King's River (10,200 ft.). Looking to the west, the great pyramid of Arrow Peak sits in front of the Monarch Divide. To the east, the broad saddle of Taboose Pass (11,400 ft.) offers the best route down to the Owen's Valley.

A long, gentle climb takes you along the South Fork of the Kings River into the huge Upper Basin (11,200 ft.). On the east margin of the basin, the north slopes of Split Mountain (14,058 ft.) offer a long ski descent. To the north lies

Looking west from Palisades Basin.

Photo: John Moynier

the steep climb to Mather Pass (12,100 ft.), which may involve a cornice at the top. The north side of the pass begins steeply, but soon becomes more gentle, providing a great run down to the bench above the Palisade Lakes (11,200 ft.). From here, you can exit over Southfork Pass (12,600 ft.) out to Glacier Lodge (7,600 ft.).

Our route, however, continues down to the west end of lower Palisade Lake (10,600 ft.) and along the base of the spectacular western escarpment of the Palisades. An easy climb up moderate slopes leads north to the obvious saddle of Cirque Pass (12,100 ft.), then down to the lake (11,675 ft.) at the head of Glacier Creek. From here, a side trip onto Mt. Sill (14,153 ft.) is highly recommended.

Steep ledges climb from the lake over Potluck Pass (12,150 ft.) and onto the broad bench that traverses below the sheer west face of North Palisade. The view west over Palisades Basin towards the remote backcountry of Kings Canyon is truly breathtaking.

Continuing north, a short climb takes you to Thunderbolt Col (12,400 ft.), at the foot of rugged Thunderbolt Peak. A pleasant run down into the Dusy Basin brings you to the very scenic lake (11,400 ft.) at the foot of Isosceles Peak. From the lake, a moderate climb takes you to the low saddle of Bishop Pass (11,950 ft.), where there are great views of the sheer west faces of the Palisades as well as of the Black Divide looming across the deep Le Conte Canyon. A short but steep descent brings you to Bishop Lake (11,250), which lies at the foot of the great ski slopes of Mt. Goode (13,085 ft.). From here, a gentle run down the South Fork of Bishop Creek takes you past Long Lake (10,750 ft.) and out to the trailhead at South Lake (9,750 ft.).

A lone skier contemplates a sun-baked ridge.

Photo: John Moynier

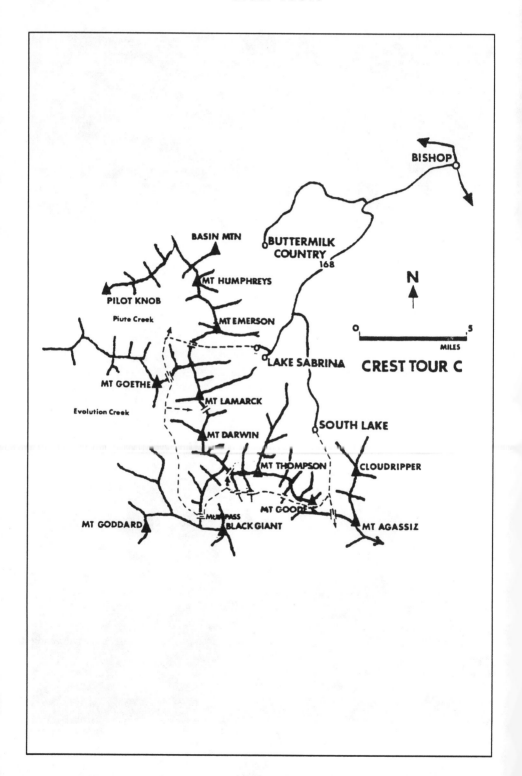

C. SOUTH LAKE TO NORTH LAKE

Difficulty: Class 3-4
Distance: Approx. 40 miles
Trailheads: South Lake and North Lake
Maps: Mt. Goddard 15 minute or
Mt. Thompson, Mt. Darwin, Mt. Goddard 7.5 minute

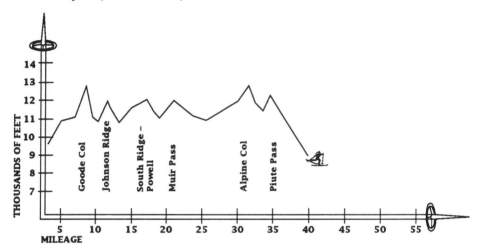

The South Lake to North Lake loop is considered the classic Sierra summer backpacking trip. This trip begins with a wonderful traverse of both the South Lake and Sabrina Basins before crossing Muir Pass at the heart of the High Sierra. The highlight of this tour is the gentle run down through the beautiful Evolution Basin and up into the rugged Darwin Canyon. This is one of the most difficult sections of the crest, but also one of the most rewarding.

Touring near Wanda Lake.

Photo: Jim Stimson

A view of Mt. Agassiz and Bishop Pass.   Photo: Andy Selters

DESCRIPTION

The tour begins at the high trailhead of South Lake (9,750 ft.) and follows the south fork of Bishop Creek up benches to the south end of Long Lake (10,750 ft.). Directly to the south, the sheer north face of Mt. Goode dominates the view. Continue along the creek to Saddlerock Lake (11,125 ft.), then head up into the cirque on the south side of Mt. Goode to the col (12,700 ft.) just south of the summit (13,085 ft.). This bowl also is an excellent ski descent.

The route drops down a very steep couloir into the large cirque west of Mt. Goode, and goes on to the small lake (11,350 ft.) to the west. Follow the outlet creek down a short distance before heading up the open slopes to the west and onto the south ridge of Mt. Johnson (11,900 ft.). A very steep cliff guards the route down to the creek (11,000 ft.) that drains the south side of Mt. Gilbert. You also can reach this point from South Lake via Treasures Lakes (10,650 ft.) and the very steep col (12,400 ft.) on the ridge between Mts. Gilbert and Johnson. The summit of Mt. Gilbert (13,016 ft.) offers an excellent ski descent.

The route follows the obvious bench system on the south side of the crest as it ascends to the large lake (11,725 ft.) on the south side of Mt. Powell. Fine ski runs lead off both Mt. Thompson (13,494 ft.) and Mt. Powell (13,364 ft.). The views down the spectacular Le Conte Canyon and of the Black Divide are some of the finest in the range. From the lake, ski up the cirque toward the west summit of Mt. Powell before climbing onto the steep south ridge (12,300 ft.). A steep gully drops you to the large lake (11,425 ft.) at the base of Echo Col.

From the lake, the route drops down to the Muir Trail (11,000 ft.) before climbing past Helen Lake (11,600 ft.) to the stone shelter at Muir Pass (11,950 ft.). This hut makes a fine base for skiing Mt. Solomons (13,034 ft.) to the south and exploring the Evolution and Ionian Basins to the west. The dark cone of Mt. Goddard presides over the wonderfully gentle slopes leading past Wanda (11,400 ft.) and Sapphire Lakes (11,000 ft.); the ski eventually drops you to Evolution Lake (10,850 ft.), one of the most beautiful locations in the entire range.

From the north end of the lake, contour around the west ridge of Mt. Mendel onto the Darwin Bench (11,200 ft.). Looking back south, the Hermit stands guard over the classic U-shaped Evolution Valley and the Evolution Basin. Lamarck Col (12,900 ft.) lies to the east, at the head of rugged Darwin Canyon, and provides an alternate exit out to North Lake (9,250 ft.).

Our route heads north to the highest of the lakes (11,900 ft.) below Muriel Peak, then climbs over Alpine Col (12,350 ft.) before dropping down into the Goethe Cirque (11,550 ft.) and Muriel Lake (11,350 ft.). The Keyhole (12,550 ft.), to the east of Muriel Peak, also provides a skiable route to Muriel Lake via the Lost Lakes (11,900 ft.).

From Muriel Lake, the huge mass of Mt. Humphreys dominates the northern skyline. The low saddle to the east is Piute Pass (11,425 ft.) and is reached by a simple contouring traverse. The broad valley below is followed past Piute Lake (10,950 ft.) and Loch Leven (10,750 ft.) before dropping steeply down into the aspens of the lower canyon, below the colorful Piute Crags, and out to North Lake (9,250 ft.).

Looking north from Alpine Col.   Photo: Andy Selters

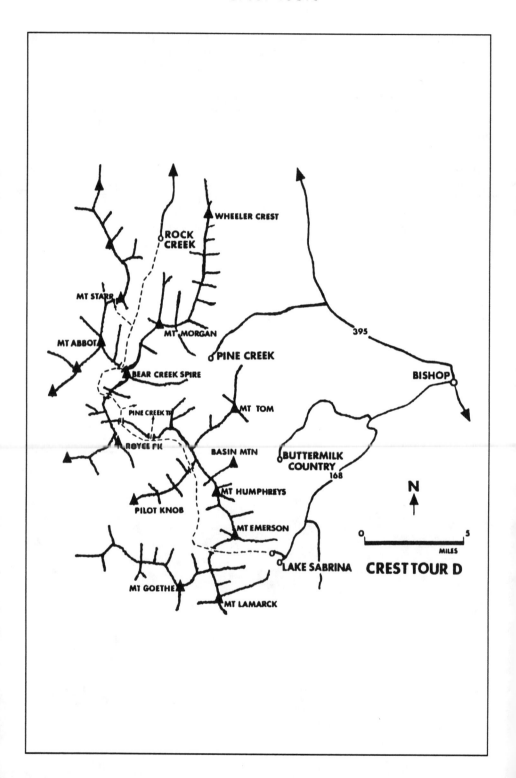

WHEELER CREST

ROCK CREEK

MT STARR

MT ABBOT

MT MORGAN

PINE CREEK

395

BISHOP

BEAR CREEK SPIRE

MT TOM

PINE CREEK TR

ROYCE PK

BASIN MTN

BUTTERMILK COUNTRY

168

MT HUMPHREYS

PILOT KNOB

MT EMERSON

N

0   5
MILES

LAKE SABRINA

MT GOETHE

MT LAMARCK

CREST TOUR D

D. NORTH LAKE TO ROCK CREEK

Difficulty: Class 3
Distance: Approx. 41 miles
Trailheads: North Lake and Rock Creek
Maps: Mt. Tom, Mt. Abbot , Mt. Morgan 15 minute or
Mt. Darwin, Mt. Tom, Mt. Hilgard, Mt. Abbot, Mt. Morgan 7.5 minute

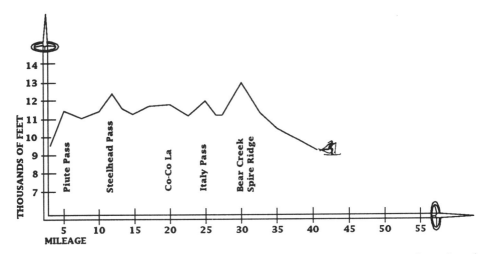

The character of the crest changes at Piute Pass. The many jagged peaks of the Evolution group are replaced by the open expanses of Humphreys Basin and the lone tower of Mt. Humphreys. The tour regains its alpine character as it passes beneath the huge rock faces of the Royce Peaks and the spectacular spires of Granite Park and Rock Creek canyon.

This is classic touring terrain and there are many options for layover days to explore the Humpreys Basin and Granite Park areas, as well as to climb the fine peaks in the Royce Lakes and Lake Italy areas. This tour also is perhaps the easiest section of the crest, with moderate passes providing very skiable terrain along its entire length.

A view of the Humphreys Basin and Glacier Divide.   Photo: John Moynier

DESCRIPTION

The route begins at North Lake (9,250 ft.) and follows the summer trail as it ascends through a forest of aspens below the colorful Piute Crags. Eventually, a short, steep traverse brings you to Loch Leven (10,750 ft.). The route follows the broad valley up past Piute Lake (10,950 ft.) before making the final short climb to Piute Pass (11,425 ft.).

From the pass, a long, contouring ski past Summit Lake (11,200 ft.) takes you around to the drainage (11,000 ft.) leading up to Lower Desolation Lake (11,200 ft.). At this point, the vistas open up to include the sheer north faces of the Glacier Divide to the south. A short climb brings you to the expansive Desolation Lake (11,375 ft.), which lies at the foot of Mt. Humphreys.

From the lake, the route crosses the low divide to the north over Steelhead Pass (12,100 ft.) and down to Steelhead Lake (11,400 ft.). A gentle traverse leads west past the outlet creek of French Lake (11,200 ft.) and on to Pine Creek Pass (11,150 ft.). The huge south face of Bear Creek Spire to the north contrasts with the zebra- striped cliffs above Pine Creek. It is possible to exit the tour via the fun descent from the pass to Pine Lake (9,950 ft.) and out the scary Pine Creek canyon to the Pine Creek roadend (7,500 ft.).

The next section is not to be missed, however. The moderate slope to the west of the pass is ascended to the stunning Royce Lakes (11,700 ft.) where there are excellent bowls to ski as well as fun descents of Merriam Peak (13,077 ft.), Royce Peak (13,253 ft.) and Feather Peak (13,242 ft.). The low saddle to the north takes you between impressive rock buttresses into the lower reaches of the equally-beautiful Granite Park. The route makes the gentle climb through this huge basin to Italy Pass (12,400 ft.) at the foot of Mt. Julius Caesar (13,200 ft.).

From the pass, the route makes a wonderful descent to Jumble Lake (11,500 ft.) and down into the stark basin of Lake Italy (11,200 ft.), which is rimmed by the great hulks of Mts. Hilgard, Gabb, Abbot and Dade. Traversing around to Toe Lake, the route slogs up the broad slopes to the north before heading east to the north ridge (13,050 ft.) of Bear Creek Spire. From here, an easy slope takes you up to the short cliff guarding the summit of Bear Creek Spire (13,713 ft.).

From the pass, the route drops into Rock Creek Canyon past Dade Lake (11,600 ft.) to the Treasure Lakes (11,175 ft.). A gentle descent takes you down the scenic Little Lakes Valley past Long Lake (10,550 ft.) and Mack Lake (10,350 ft.) to Mosquito Flats (10,200 ft.). A final descent down the Rock Creek road takes you past Rock Creek Lake (9,700 ft.) to the Rock Creek roadhead (8,900 ft.).

Looking south over Bear Creek Spire.

Photo: Vern Clevenger

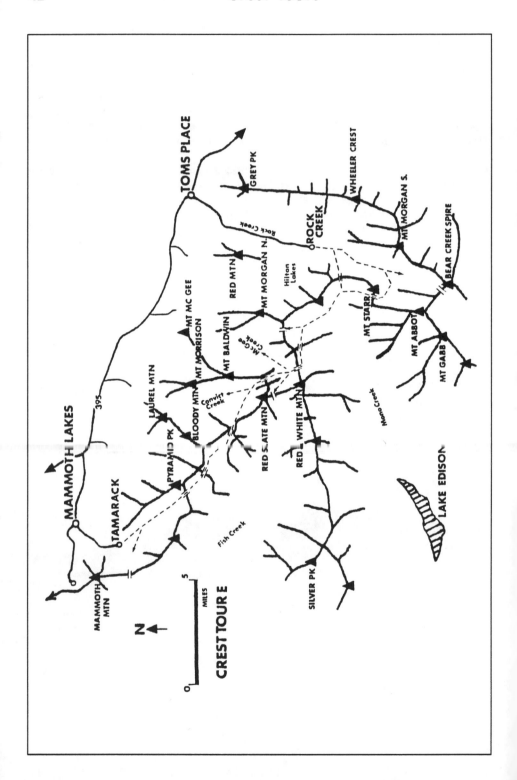

CREST TOUR E

E. ROCK CREEK TO MAMMOTH

Difficulty: Class 3
Distance: Approx. 44 miles
Trailheads: Rock Creek and Tamarack Lodge
Maps: Mt. Abbot, Mt. Morrison 15 minute or
Mt. Morgan, Mt. Abbot, Convict Lake, Bloody Mtn., Crystal Crag 7.5
minute

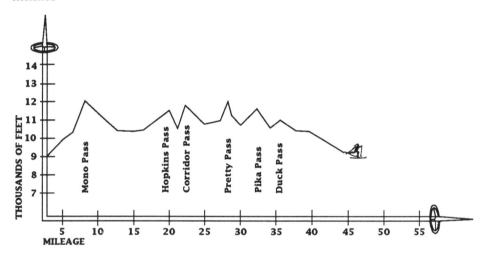

This trip offers some of the best backcountry skiing in the High Sierra. The scenery ranges from the spectacular granite spires of Rock Creek canyon to the sublime beauty of Hopkins Basin and the unforgettable colors of the Convict Lake area. There many opportunities for shorter tours in this region and alternative routes abound. The route from Rock Creek is justifiably popular, as is the tour from Mammoth to McGee Creek. This tour can be done in two days, but three to five days will give you more time to enjoy the fine bowl-skiing along the way.

DESCRIPTION
The tour begins at the Rock Creek roadhead (8,900 ft.) and follows the snowed-in road past Rock Creek Lake (9,700 ft.) to Mosquito Flats (10,200 ft.). From there, follow Ruby Creek to Ruby Lake (11,125 ft.), then circle around the south buttress of Mt. Starr to Mono Pass (12,050 ft.). The views from the pass back to Mt. Abbot and Bear Creek Spire are terrific, but the views to the north are disappointing until you begin the drop to Golden Lake (11,000 ft.). Note: It's also possible to take a more difficult shortcut from Rock Creek Lake west over Half Moon Pass (11,450 ft.) and directly down to the lake.

From Golden Lake, the route heads along the north side of Mono Creek until it is possible to traverse to the lake at the mouth of Pioneer Basin (10,400 ft.). A great side tour can be followed into the basin, but our route circles around the open south slopes of Mt. Hopkins to Hopkins Creek and on to the Upper Hopkins Lakes (11,100 ft.). There are excellent views back across Mono Creek to Mt. Mills and the great hanging valleys of the Mono Recesses. From the

Touring in upper McGee Basin.   Photo: John Moynier

A view of Red Slate Mountain and Corridor Pass.   Photo: John Moynier

lakes, an easy ascent brings you to Hopkins Pass (11,400 ft.), where a steep drop below the colorful slopes of Red and White Mountain takes you down to Big McGee Lake (10,500 ft.).

From the lake, climb steadily into the hourglass-shaped valley to the north, which leads to the well-named Corridor Pass (11,800 ft.). From the pass, there are great views back across McGee Creek Canyon and north into Convict Canyon. A wonderful descent takes you through open bowls down to Constance Lake (10,800 ft.), which rests below the great north face of Red Slate Mountain. From here, it is possible to ski out Convict Creek Canyon to Convict Lake (7,600 ft.).

The route, however, traverses the head of Convict Canyon, where you can look across the teardrop-shaped Dorothy Lake towards the colorful Mt. Baldwin and Mt. Morrison before heading west up ever-steepening slopes to the improbable Pretty Pass (11,900 ft.). A steep drop leads you down to Franklin Lakes (11,150 ft.) before making the gentle run to Ram Lake (10,800 ft.).

From Ram Lake, climb steeply toward the narrow notch where the prominent ridge joins the main crest at Pika Pass (11,575 ft.). This pass drops you down to the huge Duck Lake (10,475 ft.), before a short climb takes you over Duck Pass (10,800 ft.) and down the open bowl to Barney Lake (10,200 ft.) and Mammoth Creek. Follow the creek on a great downhill run past Skelton Lake (9,900 ft.) and the aptly-named Arrowhead Lake (9,675 ft.) to Coldwater Campground (9,000) and the trailhead at Tamarack Lodge (8,700 ft.).

Looking east from Red Slate Mountain. Photo: John Moynier

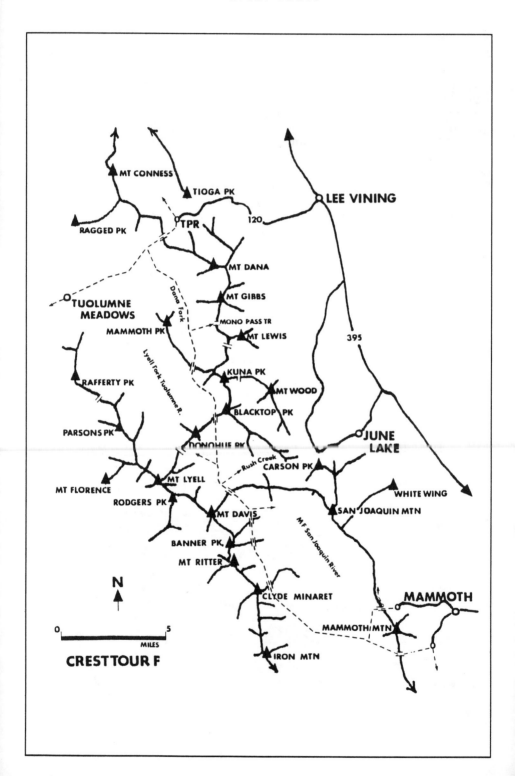

MT CONNESS

TIOGA PK

LEE VINING

RAGGED PK

TPR

120

MT DANA

MT GIBBS

TUOLUMNE
MEADOWS

Dana Fork

MONO PASS TR

MAMMOTH PK

MT LEWIS

395

Lyell Fork Tuolumne R.

KUNA PK

RAFFERTY PK

MT WOOD

BLACKTOP PK

PARSONS PK

DONOHUE PK

JUNE LAKE

Rush Creek

CARSON PK

MT LYELL

WHITE WING

MT FLORENCE

RODGERS PK

SAN JOAQUIN MTN

MT DAVIS

M F San Joaquin River

BANNER PK

MT RITTER

N

CLYDE MINARET

MAMMOTH

MAMMOTH MTN

0   5

MILES

IRON MTN

CREST TOUR F

F. Mammoth to Tioga Pass

Difficulty: Class 2-3
Distance: Approx. 52 miles
Trailheads: Tamarack Lodge and Tioga Pass Resort
Maps: Devil's Postpile, Mono Craters, Tuolumne Meadows 15 minute or Mammoth Mtn., Mt. Ritter, Koip Peak, Tioga Pass, Mt. Dana 7.5 minute

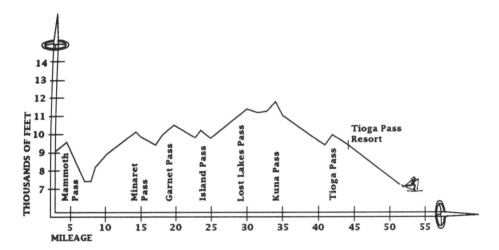

This route is not truly a "crest tour" in that it leaves the main crest to traverse the more spectacular Ritter Range to the west. This is because the Sierra Crest in this area is very low and lacks the character of the rest of the crest tour segments. The Ritter Range, however, has everything you could ask for. The scenery is fantastic and the route heads through skiable passes right at the base of the spectacular Minarets.

Although a low drop is made in crossing the San Joaquin River to reach the Minarets, a hot springs along the way serves to appease even the most hard-core altitude junkie. The route also takes a higher and more enjoyable line into Yosemite Park, catching Highway 120 at Dana Meadows, making this an fine alternative to the popular Mammoth-to-Yosemite Trans-Sierra tour.

Description

From Tamarack Lodge (8,700 ft.), follow the groomed trail to Horseshoe Lake (9,000 ft.) before climbing over the low saddle of Mammoth Pass (9,300 ft.). A fine descent drops down through the trees to the hot springs at Red's Meadow (7,600 ft.). Cross the San Joaquin on the foot bridge and follow the summer trail up through forested benchlands past Johnson Meadow to Minaret Lake (9,800 ft.). Clyde Minaret towers over the route as it climbs onto the bench that holds Cecile Lake (10,250 ft.), dropping past Iceberg Lake (9,775' ft.) at the foot of the Minarets to the very beautiful Ediza Lake (9,350 ft.).

From Ediza, climb steeply up to the Nydiver Lakes (10,100 ft.), which lie at the base of the great bowl between Mt. Ritter and Banner Peak. The east ridge of Banner Peak is crossed at the low saddle to the north (10,500 ft.), where a downward traverse above spectacular Garnet Lake takes you over another low

A view of the Ritter Range.   Photo: John Moynier

saddle (10,150 ft.) and down onto the huge Thousand Island Lake (9,800 ft.). A short climb through the trees to the north quickly brings you to Island Pass (10,150 ft.), with its great views of the Ritter Range to the southeast.

A gentle descent leads west from the pass to the forks of Rush Creek (9,650 ft.), crossing them well above Waugh Lake. It's also possible to ski in or out Rush Creek to the June Lake loop road (7,300 ft.).

From Rush Creek, follow the Muir Trail northwest until just east of a prominent knob; then follow the drainage north to the largest of the Lost Lakes (10,950 ft.). Climb up to Lost Lakes Pass (11,400 ft.) below the dark spires of Blacktop Peak and the Koip Crest.

The Kuna Crest as seen from Dana Meadows.   Photo: John Moynier

Now, you are in Yosemite National Park. Traverse the huge plateau above Kuna Creek until you are on the west side of the Kuna Crest. Kuna Pass (11,800 ft.) is the gentle saddle to the northeast and drops steeply down to Helen Lake (10,950 ft.). If avalanche danger is high, it is possible to traverse over to Mono Pass (10,800 ft.) and out via Bloody Canyon to Walker Lake (8,000 ft.).

However, the ski down Parker Creek past Spillway Lake (10,450 ft.) to Dana Meadows (9,600 ft.) can be really fun in good conditions. From the meadows at the base of this run, follow Highway 120 east over Tioga Pass (9,945 ft.) and down to Tioga Pass Resort (TPR) (9,550 ft.) where you might get a meal and a bed. The Lee Vining canyon road may be plowed to this point, or you'll have an eight mile descent to the Lee Vining Campground (7,400 ft.) to look forward to. Be aware, though, that this road can have extreme avalanche and rockfall hazard.

Skiing across 1000 Island Lake toward Banner Peak.

Photo: Vern Clevenger

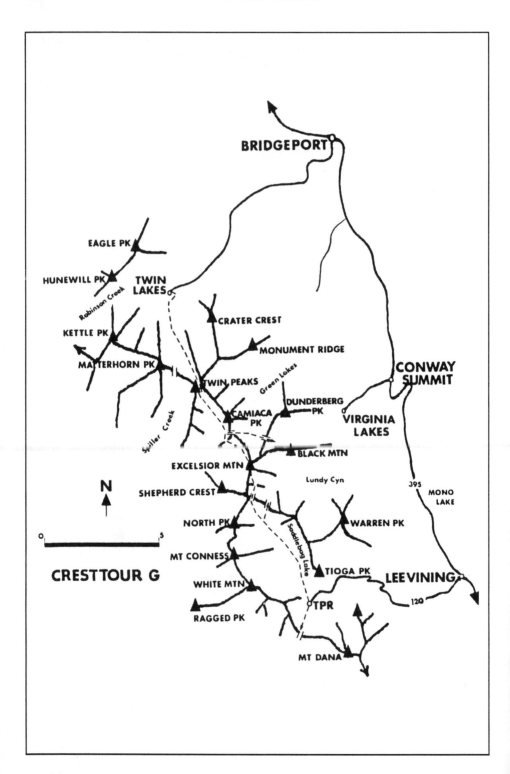

BRIDGEPORT

EAGLE PK

HUNEWILL PK

TWIN LAKES

Robinson Creek

CRATER CREST

MONUMENT RIDGE

KETTLE PK

MATTERHORN PK

TWIN PEAKS

Green Lakes

CONWAY SUMMIT

DUNDERBERG PK

CAMIACA PK

VIRGINIA LAKES

Spiller Creek

BLACK MTN

EXCELSIOR MTN

Lundy Cyn

395

SHEPHERD CREST

MONO LAKE

N

NORTH PK

Saddlebag Lake

WARREN PK

0   5

MT CONNESS

TIOGA PK

LEEVINING

CRESTTOUR G

WHITE MTN

TPR

120

RAGGED PK

MT DANA

G. TIOGA PASS TO TWIN LAKES

Difficulty: Class 3
Distance: Approx. 24 miles
Trailheads: Tioga Pass Resort and Twin Lakes
Maps: Tuolumne Meadows, Matterhorn Peak 15 minute or

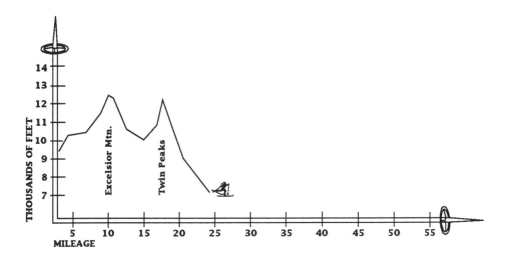

Tioga Pass, Dunderberg Peak 7.5 minute

Although this route is shorter than the other segments, it's a telemark skier's dream and has the added attraction of travelling through the little-visited northern part of Yosemite Park. There are many bowl-skiing opportunities, and the route itself climbs over two 12,000' peaks, both of which have excellent views and tremendous ski descents from their summits. Finally, the ski run down Horse Creek canyon is one of the finest in the range.

You could do this tour in two days easily, but three days allows much more time to enjoy areas like Summit Lake and Virginia Pass. It also would be possible to tie this tour in with a high traverse of the Sawtooths, coming out at Robinson Creek. Heading south, the downhill run of Excelsior Peak to Saddlebag Lake is almost as good as Horse Creek, and makes a strong case for doing this route in the other direction.

Matterhorn Peak and Excelsior Mtn. as seen from Mt. Dana.   Photo: John Moynier

DESCRIPTION

It's best to wait until the Tioga Pass road is plowed and open to Tioga Pass Resort (9,550 ft.) before beginning this tour. From TPR, follow the road up to Saddlebag Lake (10,200 ft.) past the open bowls of White Mountain and Mt. Conness. Skirt around the west shore of the lake toward jagged North Peak and the sublime Steelhead Lake (10,400 ft.) in the Twenty Lakes Basin. Although camping is prohibited in the Hall Natural Area to the southwest, it is allowed here.

The route then skirts the cliffs at the head of Lundy Canyon, following the low ridge (11,300 ft.) extending east from ragged Shepherds Crest. Traverse a huge bowl to the summit of Excelsior Mountain (12,446 ft.), where a panoramic view takes in the entire northern Yosemite Park.

A variety of excellent ski descents lead off the north peak of Excelsior and down to either Onion Lake (10,400 ft.) or Green Creek (10,300 ft.). A short traverse around either side of the prominent pyramid brings you to the stunning Summit Lake (10,200 ft.). From here, the route traverses around the

west slopes of Camiaca Peak to the head of the classic U-shaped Virginia Canyon (10,200 ft.), just below the spectacular towers of Virginia Peak.

The large black mass of Twin Peaks blocks the view to the north. Follow the righthand drainage to just below the eastern summit of the peak (12,300 ft.). A very steep descent drops down the easternmost of the two extremely steep couloirs to the glacier (11,300 ft.) below, where a short traverse takes you from the Cattle Creek drainage onto the glacier at the head of Horse Creek canyon.

This huge, natural "half-pipe" provides an all-time great ski descent to the flat meadows of Horse Creek (8,300 ft.) far below. From the meadows, follow the summer trail as it switchbacks down past Horse Creek Falls to roadhead at Twin Lakes (7,100 ft.).

North Peak viewed from camp at Steelhead Lake.

Photo: John Moynier

Mt. Hoffman appears over the Shepherds Crest.

Photo: John Moynier

Skiing below McGee Pass on the Silver Divide.   Photo: John Moynier

TRANS-SIERRA TOURS

FOR MANY FOLKS, skiing across the Sierra is the ultimate backcountry experience. It certainly is quite an accomplishment, no matter which route you pick. These tours actually are even more committing than the crest tour segments, as each definitely has a "point of no return." Once you have reached the mid-point on a Trans-Sierra tour, it's not only easier to go on, but you're in about as remote a location as you can get in the lower 48 states. Therefore, self-reliance is of the utmost importance on these trips.

The other challenge of a Trans-Sierra tour is one of logistics: How are you going to get back if you've left your car at the trailhead. Various solutions all work to varying degrees. You can do the massive double tour of California: taking two cars to the tour finish and leaving one. By driving back to the start and then skiing the route you will have a car waiting for you – but you'll have to repeat the process to retrieve the other car. A variation on this theme is to split the party in two, with half the group skiing one way and half the other. The trick is to meet in the middle somewhere and exchange car keys.

The most sure way to effect a return is to ski across one way and take another Trans-Sierra route back. There are a few easy tours that I list only as return routes: Bubbs Creek, Mono Creek and the Tioga Pass road. Each of these routes provides a reasonable overnight return back to the starting side. The last way to return is to try to combine hitchhiking, buses and walking to get back. I only recommend this as a last resort, as such an endeavor has always been an epic for me.

As with the crest tours, I have chosen to pick a direction for descriptions of these tours. Going east to west gives the impression that you are starting high and ending low, for a mostly downhill tour (this is completely untrue, however). Also, as with the other tours in this book, all elevations listed are approximate, and only are included to provide an idea of the relative elevation change of the route.

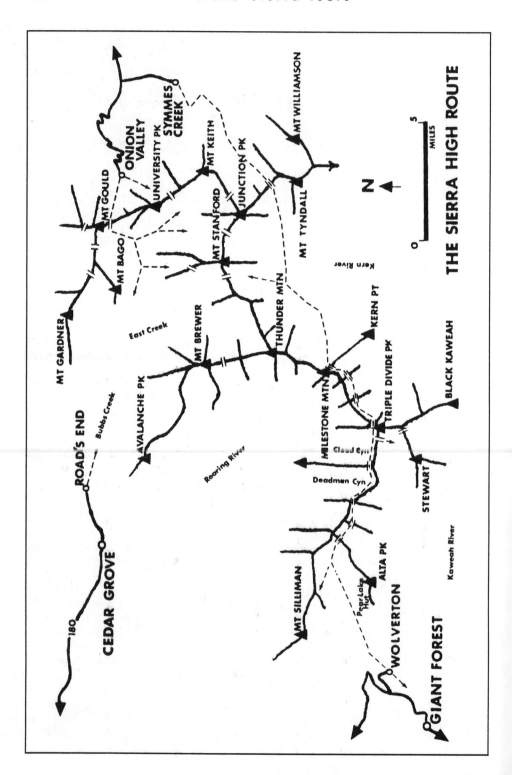

THE SIERRA HIGH ROUTE

THE SIERRA HIGH ROUTE

Difficulty: Class 3-4
Distance: Approx. 51 miles
Trailheads: Symmes Creek and Wolverton Ski Area
Maps: Mt. Whitney and Triple Divide Peak 15 minute or
Mt. Williamson, Mt. Brewer, Mt. Kaweah, Triple Divide Peak,
Lodgepole 7.5 minute

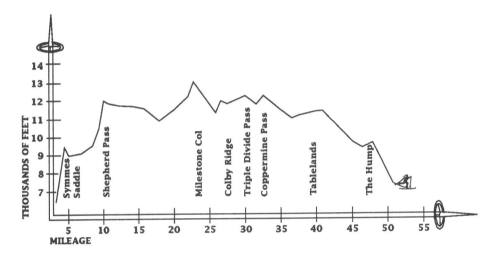

Skiing across Tyndall Plateau with Diamond Mesa behind.

Photo: Chris Cox

Sunrise in Milestone Basin.   Photo: John Dittli

This is the classic Trans-Sierra tour and the goal of most Sierra backcountry skiers. The High Route has everything: wonderful high traverses, great ski descents, spectacular scenery and mountaineering challenges. This tour arguably could rank as one of the finest ski tours in the world.

Photo: John Moynier

A view of Triple Divide Peak and Cloud Canyon.

The Kaweah range rises above the Kaweah/Kern drainage. Photo: Vern Clevenger

The High Route basically follows the boundary between Sequoia and Kings Canyon National Parks. This boundary also is the divide between the Kings, Kern and Kaweah Rivers, and there are tremendous views down each of these great river canyons. Starting in the high desert, the route quickly rises to over 12,000 feet and stays above 11,000 feet for most of its length, before dropping into the Giant Sequoias on the west side.

DESCRIPTION

The route begins in the high desert sage of the Symmes Creek trailhead (6,300 ft.). The summer trail is followed more or less, via steep switchbacks over a saddle (9,400 ft.) into the Shepherd Creek drainage. The trail takes a downward traverse across a steep, desolate slope before reaching the creek at Mahogany Flat (9,000 ft.). From here, follow the creek steeply up past Anvil Camp (10,000 ft.) and The Pothole (10,800 ft.) to the final steep slopes of Shepherd Pass (12,000 ft.), which can be avalanche-prone.

A gentle descent from the pass brings you out onto the open slopes of the Tyndall Plateau (11,700 ft.) and Sequoia National Park. Circle around the toe of Diamond Mesa, then head west toward the low saddle (11,500 ft.) at the end of the ridge that runs south from Lake South America. From here, drop down forested benches to the small lakes on the Kern River (10,650 ft.), which lie above the river's drop into the Kern Canyon.

An alternate start to the tour begins at Onion Valley (9,200 ft.). This route leads over Kearsarge Pass (11,800 ft.) and down past Bullfrog Lake (10,600 ft.) to the Bubbs Creek trail at Vidette Meadows (8,300 ft.). From here, you can ski up the Vidette Creek canyon past Vidette Lakes (10,500 ft.) to Deerhorn Saddle (12,600 ft.). From here, you can look across the Ericsson Lakes (11,800 ft.) cirque to the steep climbs leading either over Harrison Pass (12,800 ft.) or Ericsson Pass (12,600 ft.) to the Kern River and the High Route.

From the Kern, follow the course of Milestone Creek into beautiful Milestone Basin (11,200 ft.). To the east, the 14,000' summits of Mts. Langley, Muir, Russell, Whitney, Tyndall, and Williamson preside over the canyon of the Kern. At the head of the basin is the finger of Milestone Peak. Climb toward the summit tower until you're able to traverse above the cliffs on the left to Milestone Pass (13,000 ft.). From the pass, a wonderful descent brings you down the Milestone Bowl to the creek (11,200 ft.) below Colby Pass.

The route then climbs very steeply above cliffs to the prominent ridge (12,000 ft.) that stretches south from Colby Pass. Views to the south are dominated by the imposing Kaweah Peaks, especially the dark mass of Black

Deadman Canyon as seen from Coppermine Pass.   Photo: Dion Goldsworthy

Kaweah. The route then takes a scenic traverse above the Kern-Kaweah River to Triple Divide Pass (12,200 ft.), crossing into King's Canyon National Park just north of Triple Divide Peak.

Another great downhill run takes you to Glacier Lake (11,650 ft.). Take the steep traverse around to the head of Cloud Canyon, just below Lion Lake Pass. The view down the canyon is exceptionally scenic, with the peaks of the Great Western Divide visible over the prominent spine of the Whaleback. The route crosses Glacier Ridge just north of its junction with the main crest at Coppermine Pass (12,100 ft.).

A short, steep gully on the west side of the pass brings you down into the equally-sublime Deadman Canyon (11,600 ft.). A slight downhill traverse below Elizabeth Pass takes you to the obvious Fin Pass (11,300 ft.) and back into Sequoia Park at Lonely Lake (10,800 ft.).

Spectacular views to the south accompany the route as it crosses a low ridge (11,200 ft.) into the head of Buck Canyon. From the pass, the Kaweah Peaks loom above the sheer faces of the Great Western Divide. Lower down, the wonderful granite domes of Valhalla lie perched above the Kaweah River Valley.

A convoluted traverse finally brings you to the Tablelands (11,300 ft.) and the remarkable downhill run to Pear Lake Hut (9,200 ft.). The hut is manned by winter rangers and is available for overnight stays, with advance reservations. The route from the hut is marked, and skirts the slabs near Aster and Heather Lakes before climbing over the Hump (9,400 ft.) and dropping down through the trees, following Wolverton Creek to the trailhead at Wolverton Ski Area (7,300 ft.). For an even more memorable ending, follow the ski trails over the ridge and down through the awe-inspiring Giant Sequoias to Giant Forest.

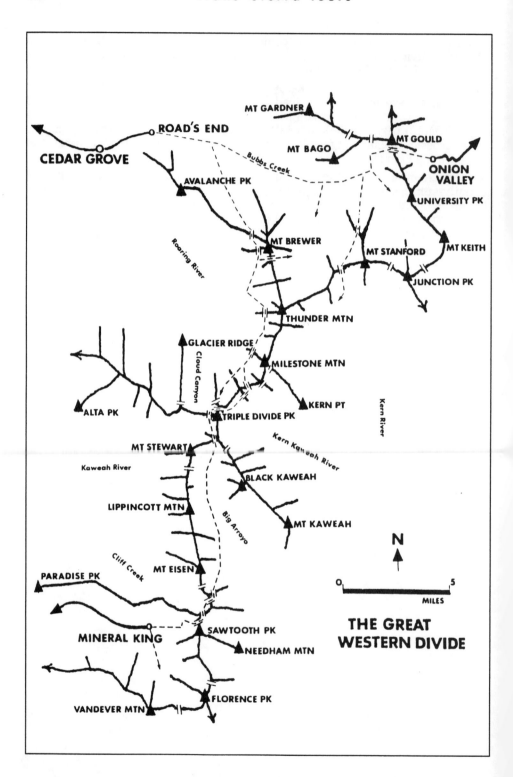

MT GARDNER

ROAD'S END

MT BAGO

MT GOULD

Bubbs Creek

CEDAR GROVE

ONION
VALLEY

AVALANCHE PK

UNIVERSITY PK

Roaring River

MT BREWER

MT STANFORD

MT KEITH

JUNCTION PK

THUNDER MTN

GLACIER RIDGE

Cloud Canyon

MILESTONE MTN

Kern River

ALTA PK

KERN PT

TRIPLE DIVIDE PK

MT STEWART

Kern Kaweah River

Kaweah River

BLACK KAWEAH

LIPPINCOTT MTN

Big Arroyo

MT KAWEAH

Cliff Creek

MT EISEN

N

PARADISE PK

0   5
MILES

MINERAL KING

SAWTOOTH PK

NEEDHAM MTN

THE GREAT
WESTERN DIVIDE

VANDEVER MTN

FLORENCE PK

THE GREAT WESTERN DIVIDE

Difficulty: Class 3-4
Distance : Approx. 50 miles
Trailheads: Road's End or Onion Valley and Mineral King
Maps: Marion Peak, Triple Divide Peak, Mt. Whitney, Mineral King 15 minute or Sphinx Lakes, Mt. Brewer, Triple Divide Peak, Mineral King 7.5 minute

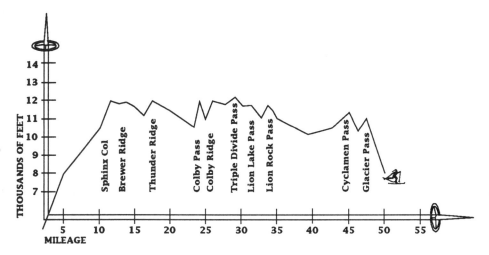

This is the most difficult long tour in this book and should only be undertaken by experienced and confident ski mountaineers. It is possible, however, to take alternate routes around the most difficult sections, making the tour longer, but a bit easier. There also are many wonderful peaks and side vistas to visit along the way.

The views from the divide are truly spectacular, as this tour cuts right through the heart of Kings Canyon and Sequoia National Parks. The tour is topped off with the descent from Sawtooth Pass into the beautiful Mineral King Valley. All in all, this is a dream tour for expert backcountry skiers.

DESCRIPTION

There are many ways to begin this tour. The classic line starts at Road's End (5,000 ft.) in Kings Canyon National Park and takes the trail up Bubbs Creek to the Avalanche Pass trail. Follow the steep switchbacks along Sphinx Creek before you leave the trail at about 8,500 feet and make the rough climb up to the Sphinx Lakes (10,500 ft.). After following the creek south to the highest lakes, a hidden pass (12,000 ft.) leads to a high traverse above Big Brewer Lake, where a short climb brings you into the hanging valley of the uppermost Brewer Lakes (12,050 ft.). The great south slopes of Mt. Brewer (13,570 ft.) provide excellent skiing.

An alternate route follows Bubbs Creek to the East Lake trail. From East Lake (9,500 ft.), climb up Ouzel Creek, below the sheer east face of Mt. Brewer, and cross over Brewer Col (12,700 ft.), joining the route at Brewer Lakes. Of course, you can avoid the tough stuff by skiing the Bubbs Creek canyon up to Vidette Meadow (8,300 ft.) and out over Kearsarge Pass (11,800 ft.) to Onion Valley

(9,200 ft.). This route is useful as a return from either the High Route, Monarch Divide or Great Western Divide tours and is one of the easiest Trans-Sierra crossings.

Where were we? From Mt. Brewer, a sweeping descent leads past South Guard Lake (11,650 ft.), down Cunningham Creek, and around the sharp west-trending ridge to the lakes (11,150 ft.) just west of Thunder Mountain. A very steep but short climb takes you onto the west ridge of Thunder Mountain (12,050 ft.). Ski down Table Creek until it's possible to contour onto the ridge holding Talus Lake (11,500 ft.).

Ski west down the creek, avoiding the sharp west ridge of Midway Mountain, before circling around to Colby Lake (10,600 ft.). From the lake, climb steeply up to Colby Pass (12,000 ft.), then drop down to the lakes below (11,200 ft.) and join the High Route. From here, climb over the ridge (12,000) to the west before making the spectacular traverse above the Kern-Kaweah to Triple Divide Pass (12,200 ft.) and Cloud Canyon. Note: It also is possible to stay high on the north side of the crest, crossing two steep north-trending ridges before contouring around to Glacier Lake (11,650 ft.) and the head of Cloud Canyon.

Lion Lake Pass (11,600 ft.) lies just west of Glacier Lake at the head of Cloud Canyon, and takes you into Sequoia National Park via a steep descent into the beautiful cirque of Lion Lake (11,000 ft.). Above the upper lake, a steep climb to the south brings you to Lion Rock Pass (11,800 ft.), which is east of Lion Rock, and boasts tremendous views of the Kaweah Peaks and the Nine Lakes Basin.

An enjoyable descent brings you to the largest lake in Nine Lakes Basin (10,700 ft.), which is at the head of the Big Arroyo. A highly recommended detour climbs up to Kaweah Gap (10,700 ft.) for its wonderful views to the west of Valhalla and the great cliffs of the Angel Wings. The gentle run down the Big

Skiing south from Triple Divide Peak.   Photo: John Dittli

Arroyo is one the great ski cruises of the Sierra, with mile after mile of constant grade and ever changing views.

Just below Lippencott Mountain, exit the Big Arroyo onto the bench to the west (10,000 ft.), and climb gently through the forests to the sublime Little Five Lakes Basin (10,400 ft.). The views from here of the Kaweah Peaks to the east are truly incredible.

From the uppermost lake (10,750 ft.), cross the ridge to the south (10,900 ft.) and circle around to Cyclamen Lake Pass (11,100 ft.), just north of a spire-like peak. Steep slopes on the west side take you down to Spring Lake (10,100 ft.). From the lake, follow the inlet creek west toward Empire Mountain, climb over Glacier Pass (11,100 ft.) to the Sawtooth Pass trail, and drop down Monarch Creek to Mineral King Valley (7,700 ft.). The road may be plowed, but more likely you'll have to ski out the road to Silver City (7,000 ft.).

Climbing over Ericsson Col. Photo: Andy Selters

Touring down the Nine Lakes Basin.

Photo: John Dittli

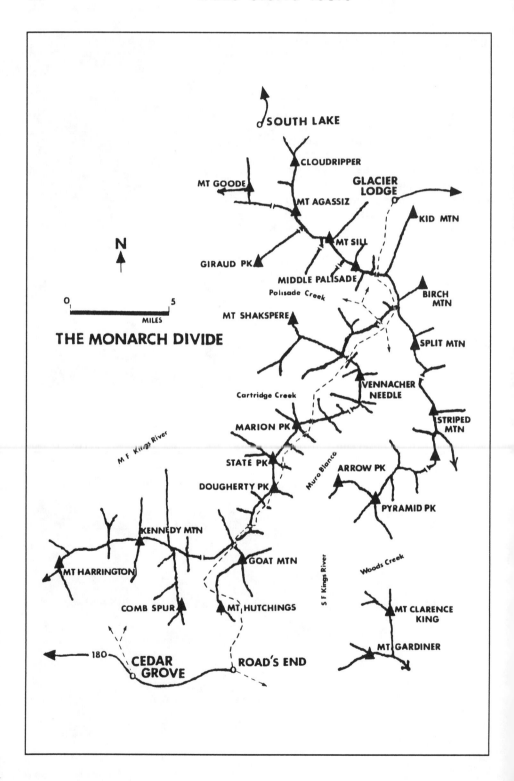

SOUTH LAKE

CLOUDRIPPER

MT GOODE

GLACIER
LODGE

MT AGASSIZ

KID MTN

N

MT SILL

GIRAUD PK

MIDDLE PALISADE

0   5

MILES

Polisade Creek

BIRCH
MTN

THE MONARCH DIVIDE

MT SHAKSPERE

SPLIT MTN

VENNACHER
NEEDLE

Cartridge Creek

M F Kings River

MARION PK

STRIPED
MTN

STATE PK

Muro Blanco

ARROW PK

DOUGHERTY PK

PYRAMID PK

KENNEDY MTN

GOAT MTN

MT HARRINGTON

S F Kings River

Woods Creek

COMB SPUR

MT HUTCHINGS

MT CLARENCE
KING

180

CEDAR
GROVE

ROAD'S END

MT GARDINER

THE MONARCH DIVIDE

Difficulty: Class 3
Distance: Approx. 47 miles
Trailheads: Road's End and Glacier Lodge
Maps: Marion Peak, Mt. Pinchot, Mt. Goddard, Big Pine 15 minute or
The Sphinx, Marion Pk, Mt. Pinchot, Split Mtn. 7.5 minute

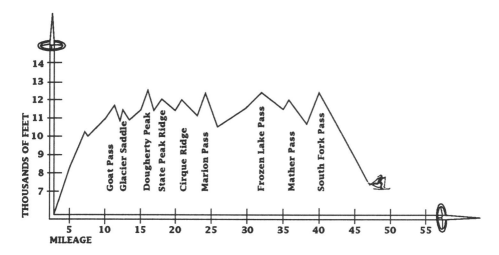

This tour really should be called the Cirque Crest Tour, as it barely reaches the Monarch Divide. However, this still is a very "regal" tour, characterized by a series of wonderful traverses linking the great cirques along the crest. The Monarch Divide/Cirque Crest rises more than 6,000 feet above the South and Middle Forks of the King's River and provides fantastic views into these deep canyons, as well as the Sierra Crest to the east. There certainly is an abundance of great bowl skiing opportunities along the way, and the tour through the Palisades provides a spectacular finish. In many ways, this tour is as fine as the High Route – and some folks think it might be even better!

DESCRIPTION
It is possible to start this tour at Lewis Creek or at Deer Cove and access the Monarch Divide at Mt. Harrington, but the terrain and usual snow conditions don't warrant the extra effort; the really fine skiing begins at Granite Basin. So, the best bet begins at Road's End (5,000 ft.) in King's Canyon and follows the Copper Creek trail up to Upper Tent Meadows (8,400 ft.). The scenery just keeps getting better the higher you go. From the meadows, follow the trail over the low saddle (10,300 ft.), enjoying great views south towards the High Route and east to the walls of Mts. Gardiner and Clarence King, before dropping into the Granite Basin (10,000 ft.).

From the middle of the basin, follow the creek drainage west of Goat Mountain to Goat Pass (11,450 ft.), which is marked by a tiny tarn right on the

An early-morning ski in Granite Basin.

Photo: Chris Cox

Goat Crest. This pass leads you down into the cirque of the upper Glacier Lakes (10,650 ft.), then climbs up to the low saddle on the east (11,250 ft.) and down to the lakes (10,900 ft.) on the North Fork of Kid Creek.

The route stays high on the east side of the Cirque Crest, traverses above the deep canyon of the South Fork of the Kings River, and features spectacular views of the Muro Blanco and the great mass of Arrow Peak to the east. Climb up the great south bowl and directly over the summit of Dougherty Peak (12,241 ft.) before making a fine descent down the north slopes to the lakes (11,300 ft.) at the base of State Peak. After crossing the lakes, the route climbs up the east bowl of State Peak before dropping steeply off the north side of the east ridge (12,000 ft.) down to the lakes basin (11,500 ft.) below.

Cross a short, steep ridge (11,950 ft.) that drops you into the prominent valley on the south side of Marion Peak. When you reach the lakes (11,000 ft.) at the foot of the peak, turn north and follow the drainage to Marion Pass (12,100 ft.) east of the summit. The east slope of Marion Peak (12,719 ft.) provides an excellent ski run after a lunch stop atop the pass.

From the pass, there are great views down Cartridge Creek to the Middle Fork Canyon, with the Devils Crags and the Black Divide forming a backdrop. The route makes a marvelous descent below an huge rock tower to Marion Lake (10,300 ft.), before swinging around to a V-shaped lake (10,650 ft.) and up into the open, rolling terrain of Lake Basin (11,050 ft.). From the basin, follow Cartridge Creek to its head at the lakes (11,500 ft.) on the west side of Vennacher Needle, then climb up to Frozen Lake Pass (12,400 ft.), just west of the small pyramid peak.

The slopes leading down from the pass offer great skiing and soon lead you across the head of the huge Upper Basin (11,500 ft.). Looming to the east is the massive hulk of Split Mountain. If conditions are right, the north slopes of Split Mountain (14,058 ft.) provide an excellent descent. There are two ways to continue: One is to cross to the large lake (11,600 ft.) and climb up below Mt. Prater to the very steep pass (13,200 ft.) near the west summit of Mt. Bolton Brown. After dropping down from the pass to the lake below (11,800 ft.), a short climb brings you to Southfork Pass (12,600 ft.).

The second (and recommended) route goes over Mather Pass (12,100 ft.) and down toward the Palisades Lakes before taking the 11,200-foot contour up to the creek that drains from the lake to the east (11,600 ft.), and climbing up to Southfork Pass. After a steep drop, a great descent leads down the South Fork of Big Pine Creek past Brainerd Lake (10,300 ft.) and Willow Lake (9,600 ft.) Follow the trail out to Glacier Lodge (7,600 ft.). Of course, you also may chose to follow the Crest Tour route from Mather Pass along the spectacular west side of the Palisades. Cirque Pass (12,100 ft.), Potluck Pass (12,150 ft.), Thunderbolt Col (12,400 ft.) and Bishop Pass (11,950 ft.) are crossed en route to South Lake (9,750 ft.).

Traversing the open basins of the Cirque Crest.

Photo: Andy Selters

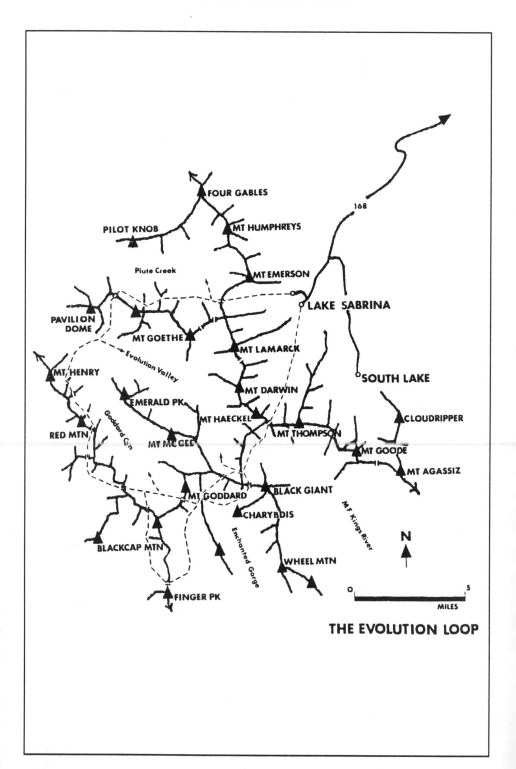

THE EVOLUTION LOOP

THE EVOLUTION LOOP

Difficulty: Class 3-4
Distance: Approx. 54 miles
Trailheads: Lake Sabrina and North Lake
Maps: Mt. Goddard, Blackcap Mountain 15 minute or
Mt. Thompson, Mt. Darwin, Mt. Goddard, Blackcap Mtn., Mt. Henry 7.5
minute

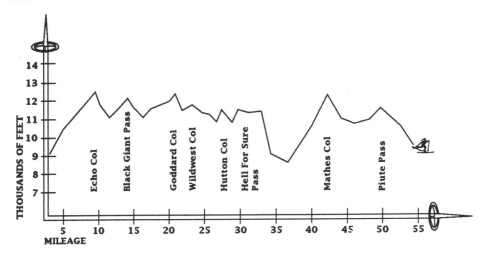

This tour really gets into the "heart" of the Sierra as it crosses not only the Sierra Crest, but also the Goddard, Le Conte and Glacier Divides and visits the Black and White Divides. Along the way, the tour traverses the beautiful Ionian and Blackcap Basins, as well as the fine meadows of Evolution Valley.

This is really two Trans-Sierra tours as it starts and ends on the eastside. This also is the most committing tour in this book, as you are at least three days' ski from any road once you reach Mt. Goddard. But if you do have the skills, this is truly a great tour into the heart of the Range of Light.

DESCRIPTION

The tour starts at Lake Sabrina (9,150 ft.) and follows the Middle Fork of Bishop Creek past beautiful Blue Lake (10,400 ft.) into the upper Sabrina Basin. The spectacular rock face of Picture Peak looms above Hungry Packer Lake (11,100 ft.) and Moonlight Lake (11,050 ft.). Continue up the drainage past Echo Lake (11,600 ft.), to Echo Col (12,450 ft.) just east of the sharp Clyde Spires.

At the pass you enter Kings Canyon National Park, and there are tremendous views of Le Conte Canyon and the Black Divide. A fine run takes you south past the large lake (11,500 ft.) and down to the Muir Trail (11,000 ft.) before climbing back up to Helen Lake (11,600 ft.). The route then follows the inlet stream south past the lake (11,950 ft.) and onto the low saddle of Black Giant Pass (12,200 ft.). Above is a great ski run on the west face of the Black Giant (13,330 ft.).

From Black Giant pass, drop down to the lake (11,850 ft.) just north of the

Touring across Helen Lake.   Photo: Jim Stimson

Charybdis. It's also possible to reach this point from Muir Pass (11,950 ft.) by taking Solomons Pass (12,450 ft.), just west of Mt. Solomons (13,034 ft.). From the outlet of the lake, drop west into stunning Ionian Basin and Chasm Lake (11,000 ft.) at the head of the Enchanted Gorge. Follow the drainage up and past a large lake (11,600 ft.) to another large lake in a great bowl (11,850 ft.).

Looking down on the Ionian Basin.   Photo: Vern Clevenger

Photo: Claude Fiddler

Mt. Darwin as seen from Evolution Meadow.

Climb into the hanging valley (11,900 ft.) north of the Scylla, then drop down to the lakes (11,800 ft.) at the head of Goddard Creek. The dark cone of Mt. Goddard (13,568 ft.) looming to the northwest can be skied easily from the large lake (11,950 ft.) at its base.

From the bench above the highest of the Goddard Lakes (12,300 ft.), the route drops quickly down to the massive bowl of Martha Lake (11,100 ft.), which lies at the head of Goddard Canyon and the South Fork of the San Joaquin River. This canyon provides a fine alternate route down to Evolution Creek, but our route rises up again to access the Le Conte Divide.

Ambitious skiers may wish to ski south over Reinstein Saddle (11,700 ft.) and down to Ambition Lake (11,000 ft.) and Blackcap Basin. A long day tour out to Finger Peak (12,404 ft.) provides excellent views of the Monarch Divide just south across the deep canyon of the Middle Fork of the Kings River.

Back on the route: Head west from Martha Lake over the pass (11,700 ft.) and down to the lakes below (10,800 ft.). You are now on the "wild" west side of the Sierra, and many miles of rolling, forested "woodchuck" country lies between you and the road to Courtright and Wishon reservoirs.

From Schoolmarm Lake, circle north to Hutton Pass (11,500 ft.), which is just east of Mt. Hutton, and ski down to Hell for Sure Lake (10,750 ft.). From here, a short climb takes you east to Hell for Sure Pass (11,300 ft.). A long traverse around Red Mountain and the east side of the Le Conte Divide leads to a prominent drainage that is followed all the way down to Franklin Meadow (8,700 ft.) and Goddard Canyon. A little further down the creek is the junction with Evolution Creek (8,500 ft.) at the mouth of Goddard Canyon.

A short climb east along Evolution Creek takes you to the beautiful Evolution Meadow (9,200 ft.). The huge masses of Mt. Darwin and Mt. Mendel loom to the east; they rise at the head of the delightful Evolution Valley. It is possible to follow this valley past Colby Meadow (9,800 ft.), climbing onto the Darwin Bench (11,200 ft.), then out over Lamarck Col (12,900 ft.) to North Lake (9,250 ft.). Our route, however, takes the creek to the north, passing the large lake (11,250 ft.) that is its source, then climbing northeast onto the Glacier Divide at Mathes Col (12,450 ft.).

From the col, there is a great view of the Mt. Humphreys Basin. An extremely steep drop down the Mathes Glacier lands you to at Lobe Lakes (10,800 ft.) and the bench above Piute Creek. The spectacular north faces of the Glacier Divide provide a great backdrop as you circle around to meet Piute Creek at Lower Golden Lake (10,800 ft.). A gentle climb then takes you up to Piute Pass (11,425 ft.) and the pleasant descent down the canyon to North Lake (9,250 ft.). A short walk down the road brings you back to Lake Sabrina.

Camping below the north side of Glacier Divide.

Photo: John Moynier

Day touring below Mt. Dade prompts a group smile.

Photo: John Moynier

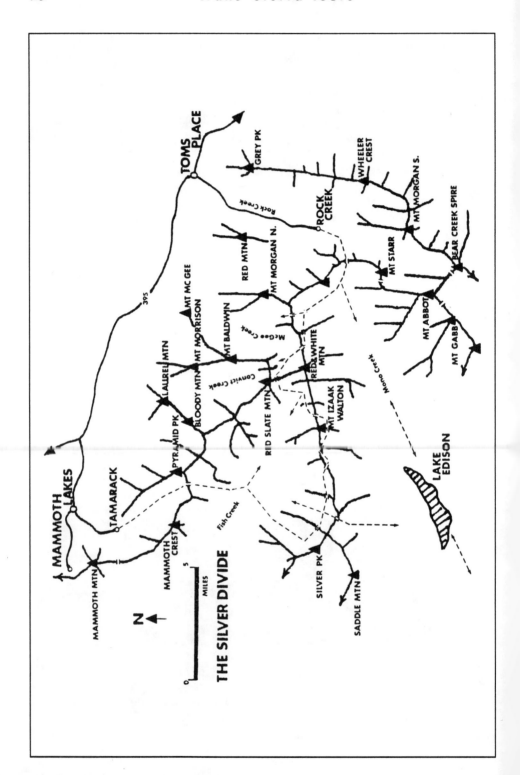

THE SILVER DIVIDE

THE SILVER DIVIDE

Difficulty: Class 3-4
Distance: Approx. 41 miles
Trailheads: Rock Creek and Tamarack Lodge
Maps: Mt. Morgan, Mt. Abbot, Mt. Morrison 15 minute or
Mt. Morgan, Mt. Abbot, Graveyard Peak, Bloody Mtn., Crystal Crag 7.5 minute

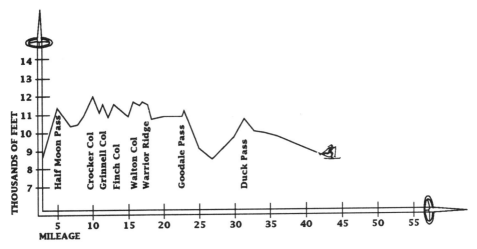

The Silver Divide is quite prominent from Mammoth Mountain. It runs almost exactly east-to-west and separates two of the main tributaries of the San Joaquin River: Mono Creek and Fish Creek. While the Silver Divide has neither the altitude of its brethren tours to the south, nor the attraction of a National Park, its charm includes beautiful country and quality skiing.

The Silver Divide is a surprisingly rugged range. As a result, there are many very steep passes and ridge crossings. There also are some great ski peaks along the way, including Red Slate Peak, Mt. Isaak Walton and Graveyard Peak. You also have the option of exiting to Mammoth or Lake Edison, and either returning up Mono Creek to the start or continuing on to Huntington Lake for a true Trans-Sierra tour.

DESCRIPTION

This route begins at the Rock Creek trailhead (8,900 ft.) and skis up the road to just above Rock Creek Lake (9,700 ft.). Head west toward the prominent avalanche cone at the base of Pointless Peak before contouring into the broad bowl north of Mt. Starr (10,800 ft.). A short but very steep climb brings you to Half Moon Pass (11,450 ft.). A short downclimb leads to a steep gully that drops you out onto Golden Lake (11,000 ft.). Circle west, high above Golden Creek, until it's possible to head north into the broad expanses of Pioneer Basin (10,900 ft.).

From the lake at the head of the basin (11,200 ft.), climb up to the narrow col (12,000 ft.), just south of the summit of Mt. Crocker, then head down to the Upper Hopkins Lakes (11,100 ft.). Crossing the sharp spur of Red and White Mountain to the southwest is steep and tricky. Climb to the higher notch

(11,600 ft.) above the saddle on the ridge, then drop down steep slopes to the large Grinnell Lake (10,800 ft.). From the lake, cross the narrow ridge (11,250 ft.) to the west, where you'll find Rosy Finch (10,800 ft.) and Bighorn Lake (10,850 ft.).

It is possible to avoid these passes by following Hopkins Creek up to Hopkins Pass (11,400 ft.) and dropping down to Big McGee Lake (10,500 ft.). Climb over McGee Pass (11,800 ft.), below Red Slate Peak, before making the great run down to Tully Lake (10,500 ft.). Follow the drainage south over the low saddle (11,250 ft.) to Bighorn Lake (10,850 ft.) and rejoin the route. From Tully Lake, it's also possible to follow Fish Creek to Tully Hole, then take the Muir Trail past Virginia Lake to Duck Lake and out over Duck Pass to Mammoth.

From Bighorn Lake, our route climbs towards Mt. Izaak Walton and crosses high on the mountain's southeast ridge (11,750 ft.), traversing the great south and west slopes of the peak to the saddle (11,600 ft.) that lies just northeast of a pyramidal peak. From the saddle, drop down to Warrior Lake (10,700 ft.), which lies below Silver Pass.

From here, you may decide to ski down Cascade Valley to the Purple Creek trail, or to follow the trail west to Goodale Pass (11,000 ft.). To stay on the route, from the pass, hold a convoluted contour above Wilbur May Lake until it's possible to drop down to Peter Pande Lake (10,000 ft.), which sits below the marvelous ski slope of the Tombstone. Graveyard Peak (11,500 ft.) also provides an excellent descent to Anne Lake (10,200 ft.).

Touring in the Hopkins Basin.   Photo: John Moynier

Touring near Duck Lake.

Photo: Andy Selters

From Peter Pande Lake, the route heads down Minnow Creek to Cascade Valley (8,400 ft.), up the trail past Duck Lake (10,475 ft.), then out over Duck Pass (10,800 ft.) to Mammoth Creek and Tamarack Lodge (8,700 ft.). You also can ski out to Silver Peak (11,878 ft.) and make the descent down Long Canyon. If you're not ready to head home yet, you can drop over the pass (10,700 ft.) to the Graveyard Lakes (10,300 ft.), then whistle past Graveyard Meadows (8,850 ft.) and down to Mono Creek at Lake Edison (7,650 ft.).

From Edison, you have two options: If you are heading west, take the long road past Mono Hot Springs (6,500 ft.) and up over Kaiser Pass (9,000 ft.) to Huntington Lake (7,000 ft.). If you are heading back east, follow Mono Creek as it slowly climbs back up past Golden Lake (11,000 ft.) to Half Moon Pass (11,450 ft.) and out to Rock Creek (8,900 ft.).

A long, mostly downhill Trans-Sierra tour also can be made by leaving Rock Creek Canyon, heading over Mono Pass (12,000 ft.), then skiing down the gentle Mono Creek Canyon to Lake Edison. From Edison, take the Kaiser Pass Road out to Huntington Lake (7,000 ft.). This tour makes a great introduction to Trans-Sierra skiing, while eliminating most of the difficulties of other tours in this book.

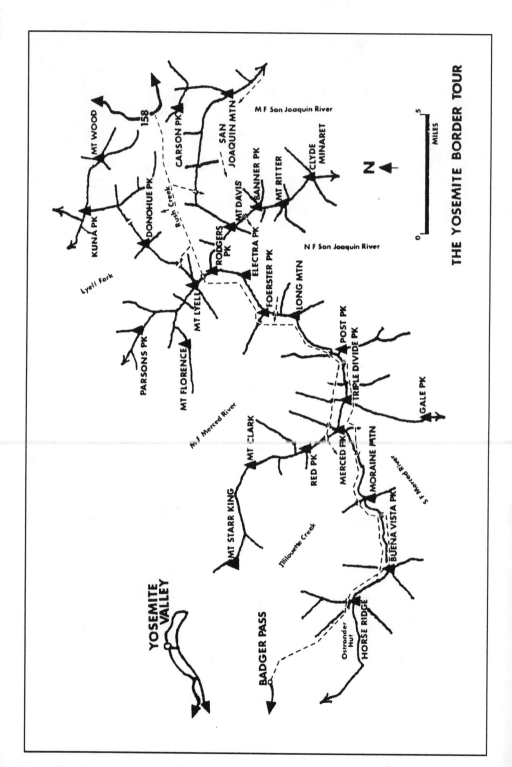

THE YOSEMITE BORDER TOUR

The Yosemite Border Tour

Difficulty: Class 3
Distance: Approx. 50 miles
Trailheads: Rush Creek and Badger Pass
Maps: Devils Postpile, Tuolumne Meadows, Merced Peak, Yosemite 15
minute or June Lake, Mt. Ritter, Mt. Lyell, Merced Peak, Sing Peak, Half
Dome 7.5 minute

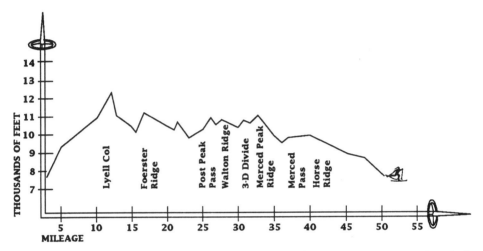

This tour also is known as the "Yosemite High Route" and rivals the High Route as one of the Sierra's best ski tours. It certainly has everything you could ask for: outrageous scenery, excellent skiing, a number of alternatives and some truly fine peaks for ski descents.

The route has many things in common with the High Route. It follows the border of a national park; it weaves its way along the top of a divide separating two major rivers (the Merced and the San Joaquin); and it finishes with a stay at a hut (Ostrander) and a great descent through open forests to a ski area (Badger Pass). An alternate finish to this tour takes you out to Glacier Point, with its awesome views of Half Dome and Yosemite Valley, and perhaps a ski descent down to the valley floor.

Description

The tour begins along the June Lake loop near Silver Lake (7,300 ft.) and follows Rush Creek up the steep tramway to Gem Lake (9,050 ft.), past Waugh Lake (9,450 ft.) and up to Marie Lakes (10,850 ft.). From the uppermost lake (11,200 ft.), climb up the small glacier and onto the steep pass (12,500 ft.), crossing the southeast ridge of Mt. Lyell.

From Mt. Lyell, the route drops down the Lyell Fork of the Merced River past the large lake (11,300 ft.) just west of Rodgers Peak. The classic "stairstep" lakes below are followed to the inlet of the lowest lake (10,200 ft.), which lies just northwest of Mt. Ansel Adams. Cross the steep north spur (11,200 ft.) of Foerster Peak before traversing around the west side of the mountain to the lake (10,900 ft.) at the head of Foerster Creek. A great downhill run leads to Harriet Lake (10,250 ft.), which sits below Long Mountain.

A view of the headwaters of the Lyell Fork of the Merced River.   Photo: Vern Clevenger

It also is possible to reach this point from Mammoth Mountain via Thousand Island Lake (9,800 ft.) and North Glacier Pass (11,150 ft.), continuing to Lake Catherine (11,050 ft.). A tricky contour route drops through the headwaters of the North Fork of the San Joaquin and across to the Twin Island Lakes (9,800

Touring on the west side of Long Mountain.   Photo: Vern Clevenger

The Minarets as seen from the west. Photo: Vern Clevenger

ft.). From here, the beautiful Bench Canyon is followed past Blue Lake (10,500 ft.), crossing the low ridge to the west (11,300 ft.) and dropping down to Harriet Lake.

From the lake, follow the obvious bench system above the Triple Peak Fork until just west of Isberg Peak, then head south and up to Post Peak Pass (10,800 ft.). Follow the ridge above Post Lakes and around the north side of the small peak before heading down to Walton Lake (10,400 ft.). Cross the south ridge of Triple Divide Peak at the obvious saddle (10,800 ft.) and circle around until you can cross the south ridge (11,100 ft.) of Merced Peak. Upper

Looking east from the Buena Vista Crest. Photo: Vern Clevenger

Illilouette Creek provides a great ski down to Upper Merced Pass Lake (9,000 ft.), where a short climb back up brings you to Merced Pass (9,300 ft.).

Depending on snow conditions, you might choose to circle along the north or south side of the Buena Vista Crest; either way offers easy touring. Stay north of Buena Vista Peak, crossing over Horse Ridge (9,400 ft.) before descending to the hut at Ostrander Lake (8,500 ft.). From the hut, there are a variety of marked trails out to the Glacier Point road; the most straightforward follows Horizon Ridge down to Mono Meadow (6,800 ft.). A gentle ski along the road quickly brings you to the roadend at Badger Pass Ski Area (7,400 ft.).

You also might want to ski out the road to Glacier Point (7,200 ft.), where there are excellent views. It's possible to ski down to the valley floor (4,000 ft.) via the Panorama trail to Nevada and Vernal Falls. Expert skiers might like to try the very steep and exposed Le Conte gully, which drops straight down from Glacier Point.

Tenaya Canyon as seen from Glacier Point.   Photo: Chris Falkenstein

A skier descends a wide-open face.

Photo: John Moynier

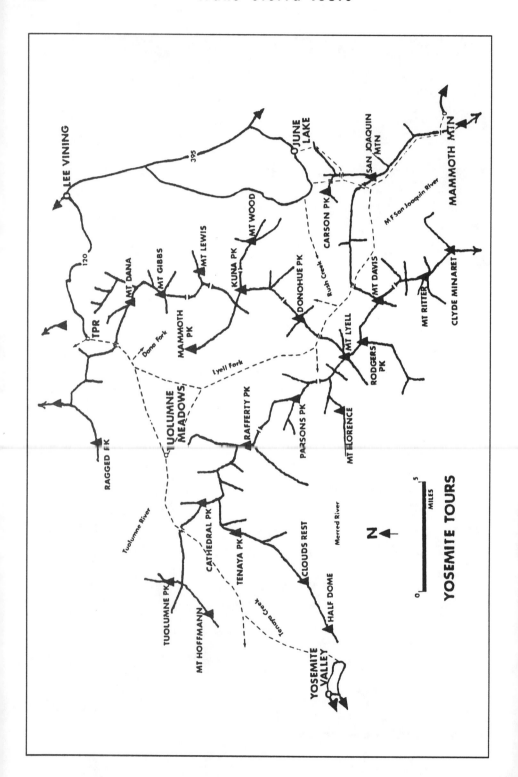

YOSEMITE TOURS

YOSEMITE TOURS

Difficulty: Class 2-3
Distance: Approx. 41 miles
Trailheads: Mammoth Mtn. and Yosemite Valley
Maps: Devils Postpile, Mono Craters, Tuolumne Meadows, Yosemite 15 minute or Mammoth Mtn., Mt. Ritter, Koip Peak, Vogelsang Peak, Tioga Pass, Tenaya Lake, Yosemite Falls 7.5 minute

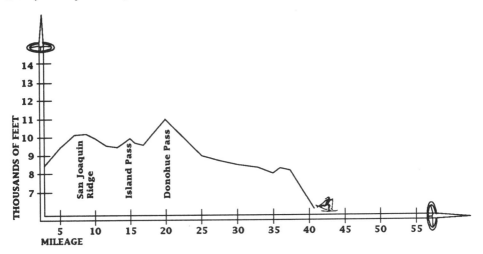

The Trans-Sierra tour from Mammoth to Yosemite Valley is probably the most popular backcountry tour in the Sierra and it's easy to see why. The skiing terrain is remarkably moderate, as the route winds its way past the spectacular Minarets into Yosemite National Park, below the granite domes of Tuolumne Meadows and finally descends into the grand Yosemite Valley.

There are many other popular tours in the Yosemite high country. The easiest is the traverse of Highway 120 from Tioga Pass to Crane Flat or Yosemite Valley. Mono Pass also can be used if avalanche hazards make the Lee Vining canyon approach unsafe. The Tuolumne Meadows area also is a great place for a base camp, with a winterized hut and Park Service rangers on duty all winter.

DESCRIPTION

This route begins at Mammoth Mountain Ski Area (9,000 ft.), and after a short jaunt west to Minaret Summit (9,200 ft.), begins heading north along the San Joaquin Ridge. This windswept ridge is a notoriously bad spot to be caught in a white-out, so be prepared. Also, be careful of the monstrous cornices that form along the ridge in the vicinity of Deadman Pass (9,800 ft.).

From the pass, the route parallels the Pacific Crest Trail along a shelf below the summits of Two Teats and San Joaquin Mountain. You can continue along the PCT to Agnew Pass (9,900 ft.), which provides access to lower Rush Creek and the June Lake loop. Our route follows the PCT to the east end of beautiful Thousand Island Lake (9,800 ft.). There are many good campsites on the north side of the lake, and the views of Banner Peak and Mt. Ritter are truly breathtaking.

From the lake, follow the Muir Trail over the low saddle of Island Pass (10,250 ft.) and make a delightful descent into the Rush Creek drainage. After crossing the forks of Rush Creek (9,650 ft.), head up gentle slopes to Donohue Pass (11,050 ft.) and the border of Yosemite National Park. A wonderful descent brings you to the floor of Lyell Canyon (9,600 ft.), where a long flat ski through meadows along the Lyell Fork of the Tuolumne River eventually leads you to the ranger station at Tuolumne Meadows (8,600 ft.). This section can be very wet in late spring and can take much longer than expected.

From Tuolumne Meadows, the route follows snowbound Highway 120 as it weaves through the world-famous domes and along the shore of Tenaya Lake (8,150 ft.). Beyond the lake, the route traverses potentially dangerous slabs as it climbs to Olmstead Point (8,400 ft.) and the Snow Creek Trail, which leads to the valley rim (6,700 ft.). The views of Half Dome and Yosemite Valley make a fantastic climax to your tour as you hike down the switchbacks past the booming Snow Creek Falls to the valley floor (4,000 ft.).

If you are heading back to the east side of the range, you may prefer to traverse east from the top of Donohue Pass and circle below Blacktop and Kuna Peaks, before dropping over Kuna Pass (11,800 ft.) and down to Helen Lake (10,950 ft.). From Helen Lake, a delightful run brings you out to Dana Meadows (9,600 ft.) and then up to Tioga Pass (9,945 ft.). A short drop down

Mt. Ritter and Banner Peak as seen from Island Pass.   Photo: Dave Page

Skiing over Donahue Pass.

Photo: Dion Goldsworthy

the eastside brings you to Tioga Pass Resort (9,550 ft.); the road may be plowed from here. Mono Pass (10,700 ft.) also can be used.

Skiing Highway 120 over Tioga Pass to Tuolumne Meadows and on to the Valley from Tioga Pass Resort is an even easier Trans-Sierra route. Crane Flat (6,200 ft.) may be also used as a higher trailhead when going from west to east.

Short tours lead to great bowls.

Photo: John Moynier

SELECTED SHORT TOURS

SOME OF THE FINEST TOURS in the Sierra really don't go anywhere at all. Perhaps they head a few miles into a fine base camp with a spectacular view or excellent bowl skiing. Maybe they traverse around a peak standing in the center of an open drainage, or head straight to the base of a fine ski descent. You don't need to travel across or through the Sierra to see some wonderful country.

These shorter tours make great weekend trips. For most folks, these tours are the best introduction to skiing the High Sierra. First of all, they start and end at the same place, making logistics much easier. Second, because the daily mileage needn't be so great, you can carry more luxuries. Best of all, you don't need to feel guilty about lingering in a fine area when you really should be getting on down the trail. You're already where you want to be.

Short spring tours and base camps long have been a Sierra tradition and they are a great way to gain experience for longer tours. Again, these selections are just an introduction to the endless number of possibilities. As with the other tours in this book, the elevations I have listed are approximate, and only are included to provide an idea of relative elevation gain and loss.

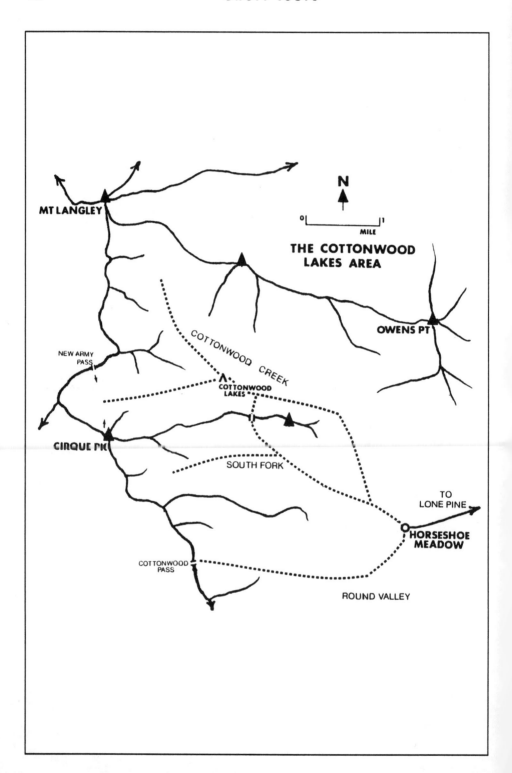

N

0 1
MILE

THE COTTONWOOD LAKES AREA

MT LANGLEY

OWENS PT

NEW ARMY PASS

COTTONWOOD CREEK

COTTONWOOD LAKES

CIRQUE PK

SOUTH FORK

TO LONE PINE

HORSESHOE MEADOW

COTTONWOOD PASS

ROUND VALLEY

1. THE COTTONWOOD LAKES AREA

Trailhead: Horseshoe Meadow
Distance: Approx. 13 miles
Difficulty: Class 2
Maps: Cirque Peak, Mount Langley 7.5 minute

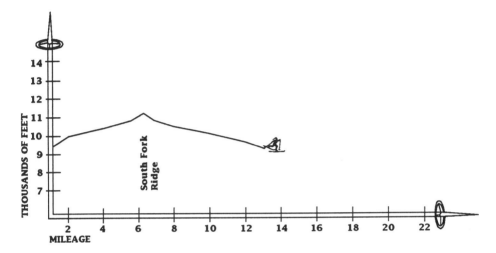

This tour is a great introduction to backcountry ski touring, combining a high trailhead with very gentle terrain. Once in the Cottonwood Lakes Basin, the views are alpine and there are many opportunities for day tours and bowl skiing. It's also possible to ski to the summit of Mt. Langley from a base camp at Cottonwood Lakes, or to tour over Cottonwood Pass into the prime nordic terrain of Big Whitney Meadows.

DESCRIPTION

The tour begins at Horseshoe Meadow (9,600 ft.) and follows the gentle valley of Cottonwood Creek north past the buildings of the Golden Trout camp before turning west and ascending into Cottonwood Lakes Basin (11,000 ft.). From a base camp at the largest of the lakes, head into the bowls of the Army Pass and Mt. Langley cirques for some excellent skiing. The tops of these

Photo: John Moynier

Skiing the bowls of Mt. Langley.

bowls are very steep, however, and large cornices may guard the high plateau leading to the summit of Mt. Langley (14,027 ft.).

A short ski across the forested plateau to the south brings you to South Fork Lakes (11,000 ft.). These lakes sit at the foot of Cirque Peak (12,900 ft.), which offers a great ski descent down its north face. It's also possible to use New Army Pass (12,200 ft.) to gain the plateau leading to Mt. Langley, or to drop into the Rock Creek drainage and go on to Mt. Whitney. The pass, however, is extremely steep at its top and can be very hazardous.

To continue this loop trip, drop into the broad valley to the south and follow the south fork of Cottonwood Creek as it winds its way back to Horseshoe Meadow.

Looking at Mt. Langley from the summit of Mt. Whitney.   Photo: Chris Cox

Executing pedal turns.

Photo: John Moynier

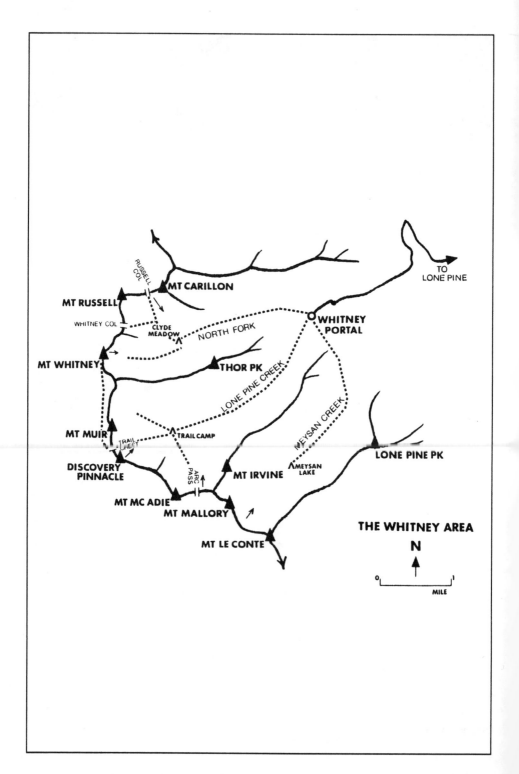

RUSSELL COL

MT CARILLON

MT RUSSELL

WHITNEY COL   CLYDE MEADOW   NORTH FORK

TO LONE PINE

WHITNEY PORTAL

MT WHITNEY   THOR PK

LONE PINE CREEK

MEYSAN CREEK

MT MUIR

TRAIL CREST   TRAIL CAMP

DISCOVERY PINNACLE

LONE PINE PK

MEYSAN LAKE

ARC PASS

MT MC ADIE

MT IRVINE

MT MALLORY

MT LE CONTE

THE WHITNEY AREA

N

0   1

MILE

2. THE WHITNEY AREA

Trailhead: Whitney Portal
Distance: Approx. 15 miles
Difficulty: Class 2-3
Maps: Mt. Langley, Mt. Whitney 7.5 minute

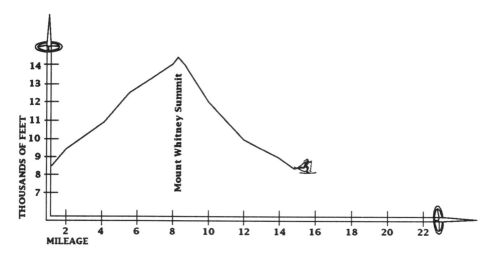

The goal of this tour is the summit of Mt. Whitney. Whitney is unbelievably crowded in the summer months, and it's much more enjoyable to climb it on skis. The crowds are gone and the signs of their summer abuse are hidden by snow. There is little else in this area, however, to recommend it as a backcountry tour. An exception is the Mountaineer's Route ski descent at the edge of the great east face.

DESCRIPTION

Whitney Portal (8,400 ft.) is the gateway to the Whitney area. If you choose to ski the Mountaineer's Route, follow the North Fork up its willow choked canyon until you can climb onto the ledges on the north side, which lead to Lower Boy Scout Lake (10,350 ft.). From the lake, continue up the broad valley to a possible base camp at Clyde Meadow (11,050 ft.). The south-facing slopes of Mt. Carillion (13,552 ft.) are skied easily from here. The summit of Mt. Russell (14,086 ft.) is a difficult climb, however.

To reach Whitney, follow the drainage to the south past a small lake (11,600), then head west toward the peak. Just below the great east face, climb north up the slope to Iceberg Lake (12,600 ft.). The Mountaineer's Route is the obvious couloir just north of the East Buttress. A difficult and icy traverse at the top of the couloir (14,100 ft.) leads up the ledges of the north face and on to the summit (14,495 ft.). However, if skiing is what you came for, you should be content with the fine run of the gully itself.

Touring below Mt. Muir.　　Photo: John Dittli

If you just want to get to the summit, follow the summer trail up the Main Fork of Lone Pine Creek past Mirror Lake (10,650 ft.) and Consultation Lake (11,800 ft.). Trail Camp (12,000 ft.) can be used as a base camp for skiing the bowls of Arc Pass and Mt. Muir, as well as climbing to the summit.

To reach the summit, climb the steep slope that harbors Whitney's infamous switchbacks to Trail Crest (13,600). From here, the route drops down a bit before following the trail along the crest, past Mt. Muir (14,015 ft.), and makes the final climb to the highest point in the lower 48 states. Obviously, there is an outstanding view, and you can see a large part of the High Route and Great Western Divide tours, as well as the route of Crest Tour A.

Sunrise at high camp.

Photo: Vern Clevenger

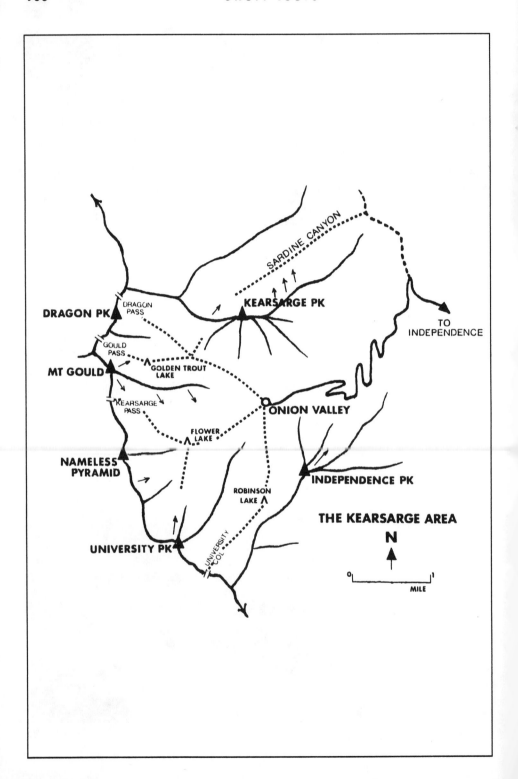

DRAGON PK

DRAGON PASS

SARDINE CANYON

KEARSARGE PK

TO INDEPENDENCE

GOULD PASS

MT GOULD

GOLDEN TROUT LAKE

KEARSARGE PASS

ONION VALLEY

FLOWER LAKE

NAMELESS PYRAMID

ROBINSON LAKE

INDEPENDENCE PK

THE KEARSARGE AREA

N

UNIVERSITY PK

UNIVERSITY COL

0   1
MILE

3. THE KEARSARGE PASS AREA

Trailhead: Onion Valley
Distance: Approx. 10 miles
Difficulty: Class 2
Maps: Kearsarge Peak, Mt. Clarence King 7.5 minute

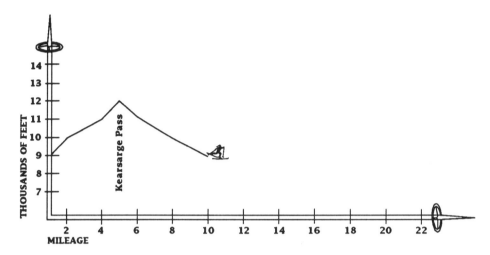

Flower Lake is one of the finest places for a spring base camp in the Sierra. It's reached by a short, enjoyable tour, and lies in a very spectacular location. The bowls in the vicinity of Kearsarge Pass offer every kind of skiing challenge imaginable and Mt. Gould easily could be considered one of the classic ski descents in the range. It's also possible to ski from near the summit of University Peak down the broad valley, from University Col to Robinson Lake. An alternate tour continues over the summit of Mt. Gould from Kearsarge Pass, and returns to Onion Valley via the Golden Trout Lakes.

Looking east from Kearsarge Pass.

Photo: Andy Selters

DESCRIPTION

From Onion Valley (9,200 ft.), follow the course of Independence Creek as it stair-steps its way up to Little Pothole Lake (10,050 ft.). An open traverse on the north side of the lake brings you to the pleasant Gilbert Lake (10,475 ft.) with its spectacular views of University Peak. Another short climb through the trees brings you to the base camp at Flower Lake (10,525 ft.).

From the camp, there are many options for bowl skiing and short tours. Late in the season, the north facing bowls below University Peak hold snow the longest. Earlier in the season, the bowls near Kearsarge Pass (11,800 ft.) are best. Great views into Kings Canyon National Park open up at the pass, with Mt. Brewer and the jagged peaks of the Great Western Divide looming to the west.

Mt. Gould (13,000 ft.) is a short climb north from the pass. The view from the summit is one of the best in the Sierra. The south slopes of Mt. Gould provide a great run down to the benches below Big Pothole Lake (11,250 ft.). The east ridge provides a continuous descent back to Onion Valley, and the steep north face drops you into the beautiful basin of the Golden Trout Lakes (11,400 ft.), which nestle below the jagged east face of Dragon Peak.

A view of the Great Western Divide.

Photo: John Dittli

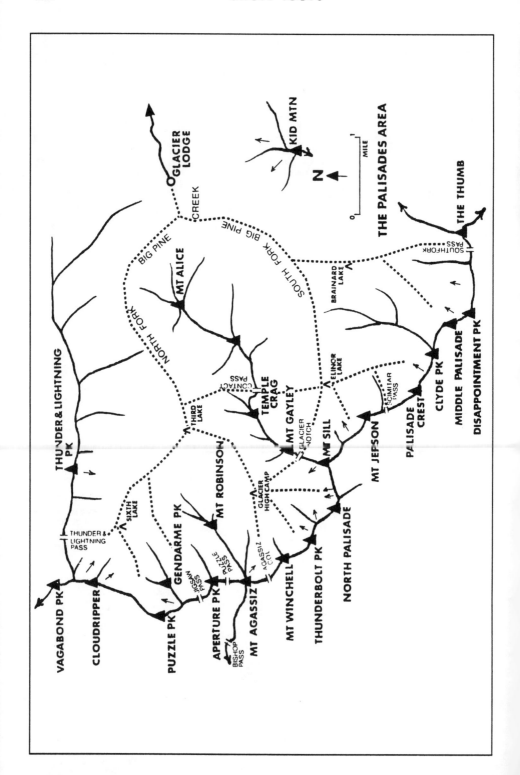

THE PALISADES AREA

GLACIER LODGE

KID MTN

N

THE THUMB

SOUTHFORK PASS

BIG PINE CREEK

BIG PINE

SOUTH FORK BIG PINE

NORTH FORK

MT ALICE

BRAINARD LAKE

ELINOR LAKE

CONTACT PASS

TEMPLE CRAG

THIRD LAKE

MT GAYLEY

GLACIER NOTCH

MT SILL

SCIMITAR PASS

CLYDE PK

PALISADE CREST

MT JEPSON

MIDDLE PALISADE

DISAPPOINTMENT PK

THUNDER & LIGHTNING PK

SIXTH LAKE

THUNDER & LIGHTNING PASS

GENDARME PK

MT ROBINSON

GLACIER HIGHCAMP

NORTH PALISADE

VAGABOND PK

CLOUDRIPPER

PUZZLE PK

JIGSAW PASS

APERTURE PK

PUZZLE PASS

BISHOP PASS

MT AGASSIZ

AGASSIZ COL

MT WINCHELL

THUNDERBOLT PK

4. THE PALISADES AREA

Trailhead: Glacier Lodge
Distance: Approx. 16 miles
Difficulty: Class 3-4
Maps: Split Mtn., North Palisade, Coyote Flat, Mt. Thompson 7.5 minute

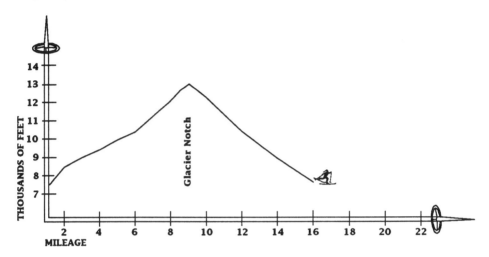

The Palisades area is the most alpine region in California. These peaks are world-famous for their mountaineering challenges, and there are many opportunities for equally challenging ski descents. This tour provides a unique view of both the North and South Forks of Big Pine Creek, and perhaps is the finest ski mountaineering route in the range. A shortcut over Contact Pass (11,800 ft.) can make this a less difficult tour. A grand circle of the Palisades also makes a great, longer tour.

DESCRIPTION

The tour begins at Glacier Lodge (7,800 ft.) and follows the North Fork of Big Pine Creek past First Falls and into the shallow basin below Second Falls (8,500 ft.). The sandy slopes above lead to an old stone cabin in the delightful Cienega Mirth (9,200 ft.). The dark towers of Temple Crag come into view as you make the gentle climb to First Lake (10,000 ft.). You'll pass high above Second Lake before arriving at the stunning location of Third Lake (10,250 ft.), which rests at the foot of Temple Crag.

From the lake, climb the steep gully to the west, below the imposing north faces of Temple Crag and Mt. Gayley, to reach a camp at the Palisade Glacier (12,150 ft.). The couloirs are only too obvious from here. Rising above the gaping bergschrund are the Northwest Couloir of Mt. Sill (14,163 ft.), the V-Notch, U-Notch and Clyde Couloirs of North Palisade (14,242 ft.), and the Underhill Couloirs of Thunderbolt Peak (14,003 ft.). Around the prominent cleaver to the north lies the north and northeast couloirs of Thunderbolt, which sit above the Thunderbolt Glacier, as well as the gullies on Mt. Winchell (13,775 ft.) and Mt. Agassiz (13,893 ft.). All of these couloirs are at least Class 4 and are the realm of the expert "extreme" skier.

Cutting turns in a steep couloir in the Palisades area.

Photo: John Moynier

Our route ascends the eastern edge of the glacier to a short climb that brings us to Glacier Notch (13,050 ft.). The great prow of the north ridge of Mt. Sill lies just above, with its obvious L-shaped couloir. From here, drop onto the Sill Glacier (12,800 ft.), which sits below the sheer east face of Mt. Sill, before making the great run down the bowl to Elinore Lake (11,000 ft.). The impressive Norman Clyde Peak lies directly to the south, hiding its north couloir and prominent rock arêtes.

It's possible to reach the west side of the Palisades from here via the sweeping route of Scimitar Pass (13,150 ft.), located just north of the jagged Palisades Crest. The route onto the Middle Palisades Glacier, however, is blocked by the wall of the northeast ridge of Clyde. Our route heads east down the drainage, joining the route from Contact Pass at Willow Lake (9,600 ft.) before following the summer trail out the South Fork of Big Pine Creek and back to Glacier Lodge.

From Willow Lake, the route onto the Middle Palisade Glacier lies to the south, past Brainerd Lake (10,300 ft.) and below the towering spires of the Thumb. From here, it's possible to circle the Palisades by continuing over Southfork Pass (12,600 ft.) and skiing across the west side of the Palisades. The route crosses Cirque Pass (12,100 ft.), Potluck Pass (12,150 ft.), Thunderbolt Col (12,400 ft.) and Bishop Pass (11,950 ft.) before closing the circle over Jigsaw Pass (12,500 ft.) and coming back down the North Fork. This is an extremely satisfying and enjoyable tour.

The Palisade Glacier as seen from Mt. Agassiz.

Photo: John Moynier

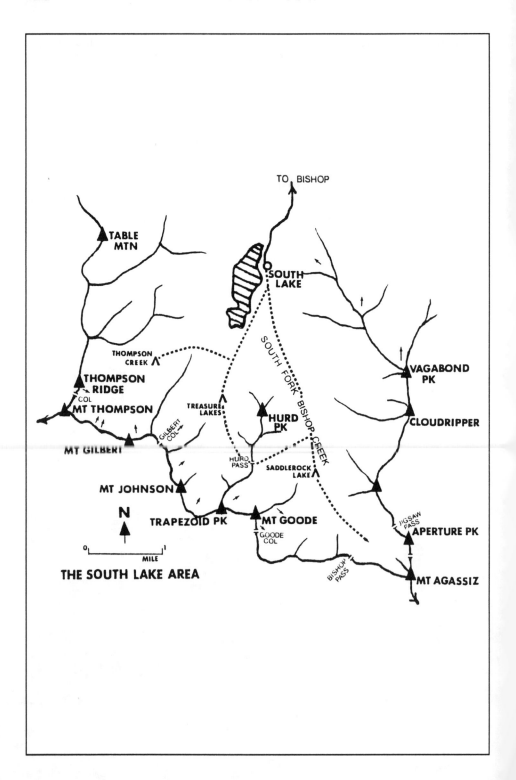

TO BISHOP

TABLE
MTN

SOUTH
LAKE

THOMPSON
CREEK

THOMPSON
RIDGE

COL

MT THOMPSON

TREASURE
LAKES

HURD
PK

SOUTH FORK BISHOP CREEK

VAGABOND
PK

CLOUDRIPPER

GILBERT
COL

MT GILBERT

HURD
PASS

SADDLEROCK
LAKE

MT JOHNSON

N

TRAPEZOID PK

MT GOODE

GOODE
COL

JIGSAW
PASS

APERTURE PK

0   1
MILE

THE SOUTH LAKE AREA

BISHOP
PASS

MT AGASSIZ

5. The South Lake Area

Trailhead: South Lake
Distance: Approx. 11 miles
Difficulty: Class 2-3
Maps: Mt. Thompson, North Palisade 7.5 minute

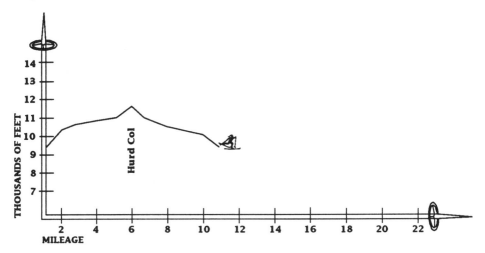

This is a delightful tour through the very popular Bishop Pass and Treasure Lakes areas and basically is a circuit of the pyramid of Hurd Peak. There are many excellent day-tour possibilities, including skiing over Bishop Pass into the very scenic Dusy Basin at the western edge of the Palisades. There's also some outrageous bowl skiing, as well as fine routes on the ski peaks of Mts. Goode, Johnson, Gilbert and Thompson.

An alternate tour takes you up into the bowl of Green Lake, which lies below the fine ski slopes of Vagabond Peak, then over Thunder and Lightning Col to the North Fork of Big Pine Creek and the Palisades.

Skiing down off Mt. Gilbert.   Photo: John Moynier

DESCRIPTION

From the South Lake dam (9,750 ft.), follow the summer trail to the bench above the lake, then follow the small valley draining from Long Lake (10,750 ft.). The sheer north face of Mt. Goode on the south beckons as you skirt the east side of Hurd Peak on a gentle climb to Margaret Lake (10,950 ft.). If your goal is to make the great ski descent of Mt. Goode (13,085 ft.), you might want to make a base camp in the last sheltering trees at Saddlerock Lake (11,100 ft.). The south-facing bowl is just west of Bishop Lake (11,300 ft.).

To reach the beautiful Dusy Basin, climb a steep gully through the headwall just east of the trail to Bishop Pass (11,950 ft.). From the pass, there are great views of the Palisades, as well as of the Black Divide to the west. A wonderful descent on broad slopes takes you through the basin to the lakes (11,400 ft.) at the foot of the spectacular Isosceles Peak.

Our route, however, contours west from Margaret Lake to the low saddle of Hurd Col (11,750 ft.). The imposing rock triangle just to the south is known as Trapezoid Peak. From the pass, you can look down into the basin holding Treasure Lakes. A moderately steep drop lands you at the uppermost of these lakes (11,175 ft.). The wonderful bowls below Mt. Johnson (12,868 ft.) are worth exploring from here, before you continue down to the largest lake (10,650 ft.).

This lake makes a great base camp for ski descents of Mt. Johnson and Mt. Gilbert (13,106 ft.), as well as the bowls below the peaks. On a day tour, the steep ridge to the west can be crossed to access the glacier on the north side of Mt. Gilbert and Mt. Thompson. This area feels like a scaled-down version of the Palisades and there are a number of very challenging couloirs that can be skied from the summit ridge of Mt. Thompson (13,494 ft.). The east slope of the high point of the Thompson Ridge (13,323 ft.) also is a fine ski.

From the Treasure Lakes, follow the creek drainage north down open slopes toward South Lake. Just above the lake, the forest becomes very dense and difficult, and rock benches guard the route out onto the drained lakebed. Once you reach the lake, a short tour around its shores quickly brings you back to the trailhead.

Touring in Dusy Basin.

Photo: Andy Selters

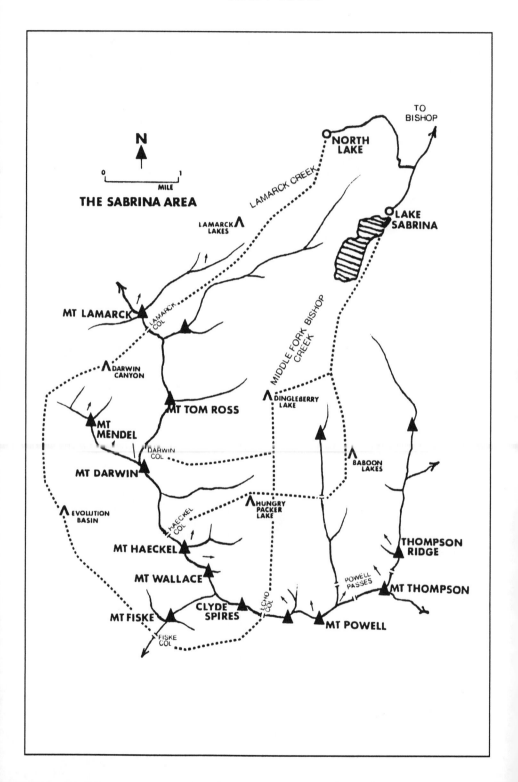

N

0 1
MILE

THE SABRINA AREA

TO BISHOP

NORTH LAKE

LAMARCK CREEK

LAMARCK LAKES

LAKE SABRINA

MT LAMARCK

LAMARCK COL

DARWIN CANYON

MT TOM ROSS

DINGLEBERRY LAKE

MIDDLE FORK BISHOP CREEK

MT MENDEL

DARWIN COL

BABOON LAKES

MT DARWIN

EVOLUTION BASIN

HAECKEL COL

HUNGRY PACKER LAKE

MT HAECKEL

THOMPSON RIDGE

MT WALLACE

POWELL PASSES

MT THOMPSON

MT FISKE

CLYDE SPIRES

ECHO COL

MT POWELL

FISKE COL

6. THE SABRINA AREA

Trailhead: Lake Sabrina
Distance: Approx. 33 miles
Difficulty: Class 3
Maps: Mt. Thompson, Mt. Goddard, Mt. Darwin 7.5 minute

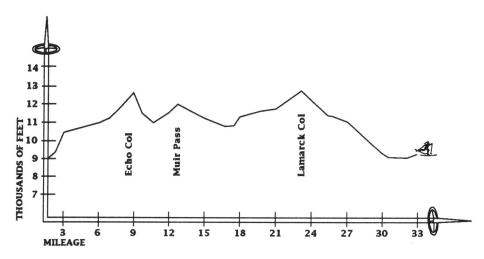

Basically, this is a shortened version of the Evolution Loop or Crest Tour C. It's a popular and very valid tour in its own right, and probably fits most folks' goals better. As with those other two tours, you get right into the heart of the High Sierra. Of course, you may just want to set up base camp at Hungry Packer Lake and explore the wonderful bowls on the east side of the Evolution group.

Skiing below Echo Col.   Photo: John Moynier

DESCRIPTION

This tour begins at the spectacular Lake Sabrina (9,150 ft.). After skiing around the drained lakeshore, follow the Middle Fork of Bishop Creek as it climbs up benches to the beautiful Blue Lake (10,400 ft.). From here, it is possible to ski south up the valley past Baboon Lakes (11,000 ft.), to Sunset Lake (11,500 ft.) and the great skiing on the Thompson Glacier. You even can link up with the main route by skiing over the low saddle to the west (11,900 ft.) and dropping down the very steep slopes to Moonlight Lake (11,050 ft.).

The main route, however, heads west from Blue Lake below a prominent unnamed spire and around to Dingleberry Lake (10,500 ft.). The Middle Fork of Bishop Creek then is followed towards the great rock face of Picture Peak that presides over Hungry Packer and Moonlight Lakes (11,050 ft.). There are many fine ski possibilities from a base camp here, including ski descents of Mt. Haeckel (13,418 ft.) and Mt. Wallace (13,377 ft.), as well as the Powell Glacier.

From Moonlight Lake, the route climbs into the great cirque holding Echo Lake (11,600 ft.) before making the final ascent below the Clyde Spires to Echo Col (12,400 ft.). A steep descent takes you past the lake below (11,500 ft.) and down to the Muir Trail (11,000 ft.), before climbing back up to Helen Lake (11,600 ft.). A short climb to the west brings you to the stone shelter sitting atop Muir Pass (11,950 ft.). This hut makes a fine base for ski descents of the surrounding peaks, including Mt. Solomons (13,034 ft.) and the Black Giant (13,330 ft.).

The wonderful descent through the Evolution Basin takes you past Wanda Lake (11,400 ft.) and Sapphire Lake (11,000 ft.) before reaching beautiful Evolution Lake (10,850 ft.). Climb north onto the Darwin Bench (11,200 ft.), then follow the contour into the classic U-shaped Darwin Canyon (11,600 ft.) to the east. From the uppermost lakes (12,100 ft.), the great north face of Mt. Darwin (13,831 ft.) provides a very challenging ski descent. The low saddle just northeast of Mt. Darwin also can be used to drop back down into the Middle Fork drainage and Lake Sabrina.

From the main canyon, a steep climb to the northeast brings you to Lamarck Col (12,900 ft.), just south of Mt. Lamarck (13,417 ft.). Care must be taken to chose the right pass, as the obvious saddle south of the small pyramid takes you into more difficult terrain and an entirely different drainage.

The descent from Lamarck Col is a classic in itself, as it follows the broad valley to the northeast before dropping down the steep slopes to Upper Darwin Lake (10,900 ft.). This lake makes a great base camp for skiing the challenging couloirs off of Mt. Lamarck and the Keyhole Plateau. From the lake, follow Lamarck Creek past Lower Lamarck Lake (10,650 ft.) and down steep, forested slopes to Grass Lake (9,900 ft.), before taking the summer trail down to North Lake (9,250 ft.) and back to Lake Sabrina via the road.

Skiing on Evolution Lake.

Photo: Jim Stimson

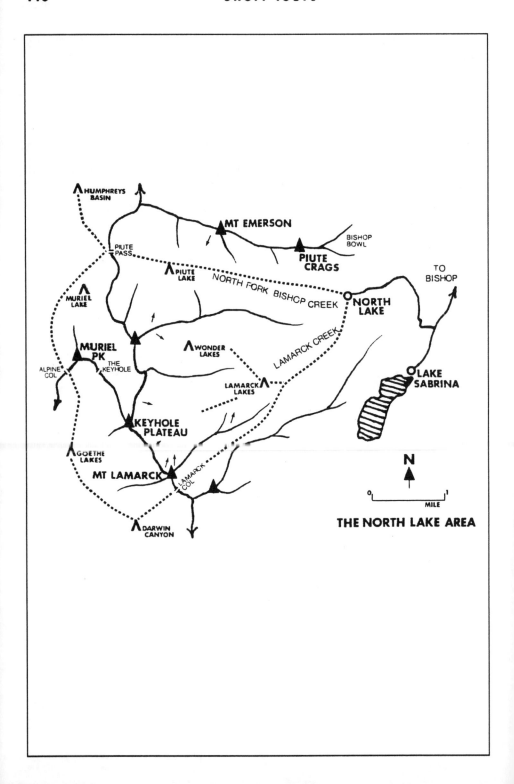

THE NORTH LAKE AREA

7. THE NORTH LAKE AREA

Trailhead: North Lake
Distance: Approx. 21 miles
Difficulty: Class 3
Maps: Mt. Darwin 7.5 minute

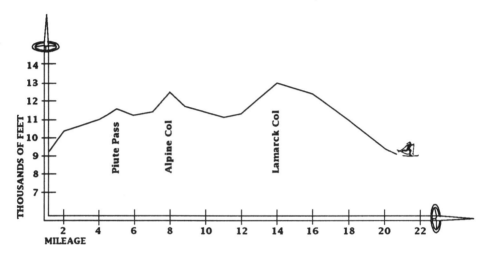

This is another very popular short tour that crosses the crest and peeks into the high country of Kings Canyon National Park. The tour follows the moderate route over Piute Pass before crossing the Glacier Divide at Alpine Col and dropping down into spectacular Darwin Canyon. Layover days allow for exploring the beautiful Evolution Basin, as well as possible ski descents of Mt. Darwin, Mt. Lamarck and other fine peaks in the area.

A view of Mt. Emerson of Mt. Darwin and the North Lake area.   Photo: Vern Clevenger

DESCRIPTION

The tour begins at North Lake (9,250 ft.) and follows the summer route below the Piute Crags to the steep traverse leading to Loch Leven (10,750 ft.). Follow the broad valley above past Piute Lake (10,950 ft.) to the final short climb of Piute Pass (11,425 ft.). A great detour from the pass leads northwest to a base camp in Humphreys Basin at Desolation Lake (11,375 ft.).

Our route, however, heads southwest from the pass around Muriel Lake (10,350 ft.) and on to Goethe Lake (11,550 ft.) in the stunning Goethe Cirque. Directly ahead is the sheer north face of Mt. Goethe, rising above the glacier. Climb steeply out of the cirque to Alpine Col (12,350 ft.) just southwest of Muriel Peak. From here, the tops of Mt. Darwin and Mt. Mendel loom over the rugged Darwin Canyon.

Drop down to the large lake below (11,900 ft.), ski past the lake at the mouth of the cirque (11,550 ft.), then circle east to the lakes of Darwin Canyon (11,600 ft.). A base camp here allows you to explore the Darwin Glacier, as well as perhaps make a ski descent of the great north slope of Mt. Darwin (13,831 ft.). On the climb up to Lamarck Col (12,900 ft.), be sure to take the saddle just south of Mt. Lamarck (13,417 ft.), and not the one south of the small pyramid, as that pass drops you down steep slopes into the wrong drainage.

From the top of the pass, follow the long, gentle valley to the northeast, then drop down steep slopes to Upper Lamarck Lake (10,900 ft.). This lake also can be used as a base camp for skiing the gullies of Mt. Lamarck and the Keyhole Plateau. From the lake, follow Lamarck Creek past Lower Lamarck Lake (10,650 ft.), down the steep, forested slopes to Grass Lake (9,900 ft.). Follow the summer trail from the lake down to the road at North Lake (9,250 ft.).

Photo: John Moynier

Skiing the bowls near Lamarck Col.

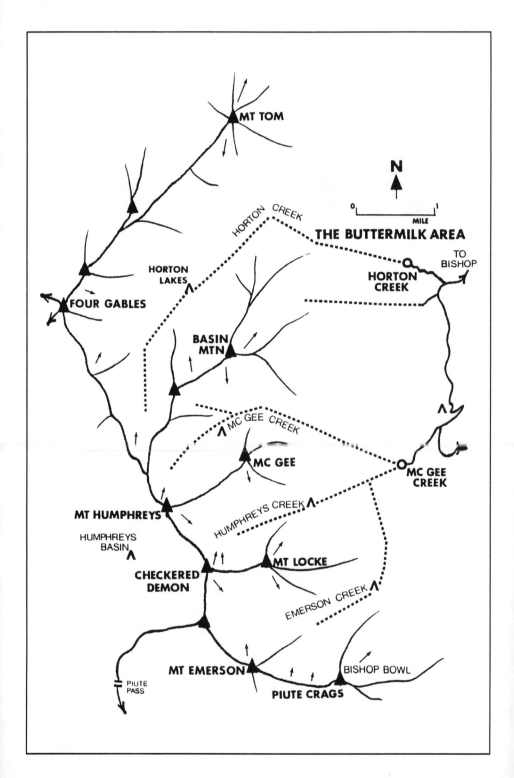

8. THE BUTTERMILK AREA

Trailhead: The Buttermilk Road
Distance: Day Trips
Difficulty: Class 2-4
Maps: Mt. Tom 7.5 minute

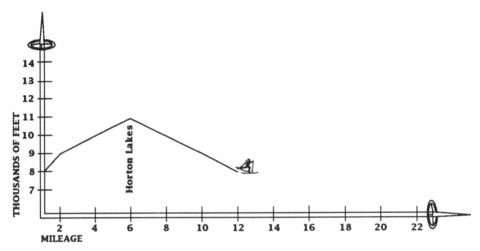

The Buttermilk area makes a great late spring base camp, as you can enjoy a great ski descent in the morning and then go bouldering or fishing in the afternoon. While these are not really tours, this area has the highest concentration of classic ski descents on the east side. Mt. Tom and Basin Mountain have been singled out, but certainly the Wahoo gullies on Mt. Locke easily could have be included, as could the Bishop Bowl, Checkered Demon and northeast couloir of Mt. Humphreys.

A view of the skyline: Bishop Bowl to Basin Mountain. Photo: John Moynier

DESCRIPTION

This area hardly needs a description as these peaks are visible from downtown Bishop. Take the Buttermilk road off State Highway 168 west, past the wonderful Peabody boulders and up into the high desert of Buttermilk country (7,800 ft.).

A rough trail leads into the valley between Mt. Tom and Basin Mountain to lower Horton Lakes (9,950 ft.). The south side of Mt. Tom (13,652 ft.) is accessed from here. There are many great bowls above Upper Horton Lakes (10,900 ft.), including descents off the south side of the Four Gables (12,800 ft.), the north slope of Basin Mountain (13,181 ft.) and the plateau (12,875 ft.) west of Basin Mountain.

Just past where the Buttermilk road crosses McGee Creek, take the old road (not driveable) up to the meadow just east of McGee Peak. To the northwest, McGee Creek leads past Longley Reservoir (10,700 ft.) and up into the cirque below the sheer north face of Mt. Humphreys. The northeast couloir is the extremely steep gully leading down from the notch just north of the peak.

The real attraction of this area, however, is the next cirque south. A base camp at the meadow provides quick access to a wide variety of skiing. To the north, the broad slopes off of McGee Peak appeal to the intermediate skier, while to the west, the hidden couloirs of the Checkered Demon offer much more difficult descents.

Of prime interest, however, are the five fingers of the Wahoo gullies on Mt. Locke (12,241 ft.), just above the camp. All of them are quite steep, but only the middle finger goes all the way to the top and as such is the most popular. The southeast slope of Mt. Locke is moderate and offers the best descent in early season or at times of high avalanche hazard.

Finally, the bowls below the sheer north face of Piute Crags also are worth exploring, as is the very steep couloir on the north face of Mt. Emerson (13,204 ft.). The east slope of Peak 12,704, at the end of the crags, is known as the Bishop Bowl. This often has really good powder in the winter and is best accessed from Aspendell (8,400 ft.) on Highway 168 below Lake Sabrina.

Looking down the Basin Couloir.   Photo: John Moynier

Skiing a finger of the Wahoo Gullies.

Photo: John Moynier

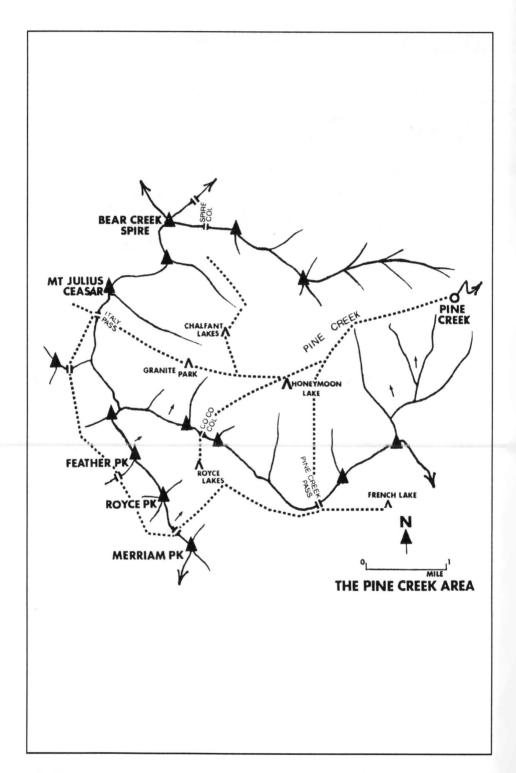

BEAR CREEK
SPIRE

SPIRE
COL

MT JULIUS
CEASAR

ITALY
PASS

CHALFANT
LAKES

PINE CREEK

PINE
CREEK

GRANITE PARK

HONEYMOON
LAKE

CO CO
COL

ROYCE
LAKES

PINE
PASS

PINE CREEK

FEATHER PK

ROYCE PK

FRENCH LAKE

MERRIAM PK

N

0   1
MILE

THE PINE CREEK AREA

9. THE PINE CREEK AREA

Trailhead: Pine Creek
Distance: Approx. 25 miles
Difficulty: Class 2-3
Maps: Mt. Tom, Mt. Hilgard 7.5 minute

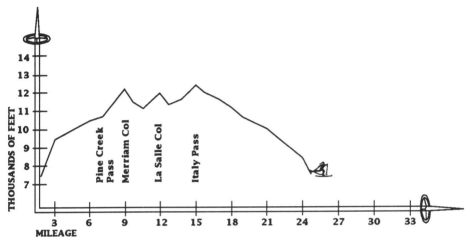

This tour takes in some of the finest high country scenery in the Sierra. The colorful rock of lower Pine Creek canyon contrasts brilliantly with the orange granite spires of Granite Park and the Royce Lakes. This tour also accesses the little-visited Bear Lakes, below the Seven Gables, as well as a possible side trip into the huge basin of Lake Italy. A fine base camp can be placed at Honeymoon Lake, or at the entrance to Granite Park. The drawback of this area, however, is that it is reached via Pine Creek canyon, which is very avalanche-prone.

Touring up to Honeymoon Lake.   Photo: John Moynier

DESCRIPTION

The tour begins at the summer trailhead in Pine Creek (7,500 ft.), below the huge Pine Creek Tungsten Mine. This is major-league avalanche terrain. The summer trail winds past the ruins of the Brownstone mine (9,200 ft.), before making a very intimidating traverse above the cliffs of Pine Creek, and eventually reaches Lower Pine Lake (9,950).

After skiing across the lake, follow the drainage to Upper Pine Lake (10,200 ft.). If you plan to establish base camp at Honeymoon Lake (10,400 ft.) or at the mouth of Granite Park (11,100 ft.), follow the drainage to the west. Our route, however, follows Pine Creek south along its gentle course to the broad saddle of Pine Creek Pass (11,100 ft.).

From the pass, the route heads up moderate slopes to the west. A contour to the northwest then brings you to the lake (11,650 ft.) at the base of the prominent granite pillar of Merriam Peak. You may want to set up base camp at the largest of these lakes (11,725 ft.) and sample the outrageous bowl skiing here. Feather Peak (13,242 ft.) is especially fine, with two very challenging couloirs on its north face.

Our route ascends the bowl between Merriam Peak (13,100 ft.) and Royce Peak (13,253 ft.), both of which are easily climbed from the pass at its head (12,200 ft.). Drop down the west side past a small lake (11,850 ft.), before heading west for the lakes (11,200 ft.) below La Salle Lake. A short, but steep climb takes you to the pass (12,000 ft.) leading into Bear Lakes Basin, where the sheer eastern face of the Seven Gables looms over the aptly named Vee Lake (11,150 ft.).

Climb north over benches, past upper Bear Lakes (11,700 ft.), and enter the hanging valley (12,150 ft.) just east of a prominent pyramid peak. From the northern end of this valley, a high traverse above Jumble Lake brings you to the final climb up Italy Pass (12,300 ft.) at the foot of Mt. Julius Caesar.

From the pass, a wonderful descent takes you beneath the spectacular granite spires of upper Granite Park (11, 600 ft.), before following the drainage past Honeymoon Lake (10,400 ft.) and down to Upper Pine Lake. The route down Pine Creek Canyon is always more fun than it was on the way up.

Looking over Italy Pass to Seven Gables.

Photo: Vern Clevenger

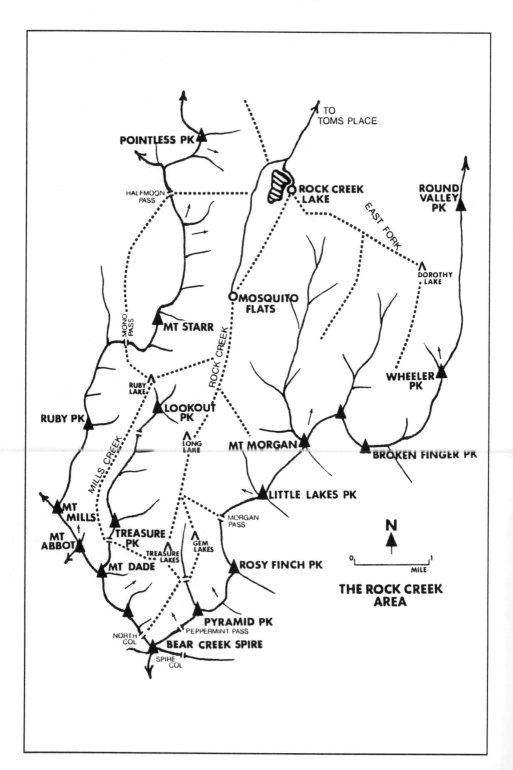

POINTLESS PK

HALFMOON PASS

TO TOMS PLACE

ROCK CREEK LAKE

EAST FORK

ROUND VALLEY PK

DOROTHY LAKE

MONO PASS

MT STARR

MOSQUITO FLATS

ROCK CREEK

RUBY LAKE

LOOKOUT PK

RUBY PK

MILLS CREEK

LONG LAKE

MT MORGAN

WHEELER PK

BROKEN FINGER PK

LITTLE LAKES PK

MT MILLS

MT ABBOT

TREASURE PK

TREASURE LAKES

GEM LAKES

MORGAN PASS

MT DADE

ROSY FINCH PK

N

0 1 MILE

THE ROCK CREEK AREA

PYRAMID PK

NORTH COL

PEPPERMINT PASS

BEAR CREEK SPIRE

SPIRE COL

10. THE ROCK CREEK AREA

Trailhead: Rock Creek Lake
Distance: Approx. 20 miles
Difficulty: Class 2-3
Maps: Mt. Morgan, Mt. Abbot 7.5 minute

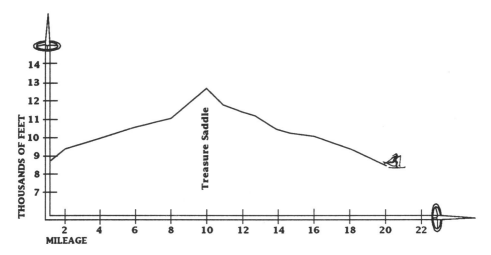

This canyon has long been considered the finest in the range for backcountry skiing. The flat floor of the Little Lakes Valley offers excellent touring, while the high glacial cirques along the sides and at the head of the canyon offer spectacular bowls and couloirs. Treasure Lakes, at the base of Mt. Dade and Bear Creek Spire, is arguably the finest spring base camp location in the Sierra.

As alternatives, the tour around Mt. Starr, which takes you over Half Moon and Mono Passes, is a great day trip for the experienced skier. Touring through the gentle terrain of the Tamarack Bench near Dorothy Lake offers an entirely different view and experience from the main canyon. Note: This canyon, like the others along this stretch of the crest, runs north-south, even though it's on the "east" side of the range.

Bear Creek Spire as seen from Long Lake.

Photo: John Moynier

DESCRIPTION

The tour begins at Rock Creek (8,900 ft.) and follows the summer road to Rock Creek Lake (9,700 ft.) below the massive avalanche gullies on the east side of Mt. Starr (12,835 ft.). In safe conditions, these chutes offer great skiing, as does the bowl below Half Moon Pass. At Mosquito Flats (10,200 ft.), leave the road and enter the classic U-shaped canyon of Little Lakes Valley at Marsh Lake (10,350 ft.). To reach the Treasure Lakes base camp from here, follow the drainage past the inlet of Long Lake (10,550 ft.) and up a shallow gully to Treasure Lakes (11,175 ft.). There are wonderful bowls in the upper cirque above these lakes, and the hourglass-shaped couloir below the summit of Mt. Dade (13,600 ft.) makes an excellent ski descent.

Our route continues up steep slopes to the west to the broad saddle (12,500 ft.) between Mt. Dade and Treasure Peak and the large Abbot glacier. Mt. Abbot (13,704 ft.), the Mills-Abbot col, and Mt. Mills (13,451 ft.) all sport excellent ski descents down couloirs from near their summits. There are two great base camps from which to enjoy these descents: The first is at exposed Mills Lake (11,700 ft.); the second at spectacular Ruby Lake (11,100 ft.), which lies at the foot of the sheer walls of Ruby Peak.

Mono Pass (12,050 ft.) and Mt. Starr (12,835 ft.) also are accessed easily from Ruby Lake. Follow the outlet creek down its narrow drainage back to Marsh Lake and out to the trailhead via Mosquito Flats and Rock Creek Lake. For a fun alternative, ski the forested knolls straight down to Rock Creek Lake, past the summer cabins and then around to the summer road at the Lakes Resort.

Looking up at Half Moon Pass from the Tamarack Bench.

Photo: John Moynier

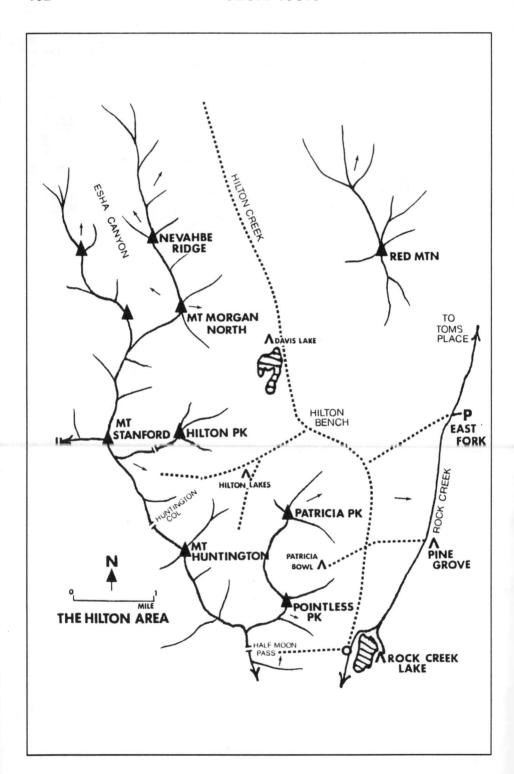

THE HILTON AREA

11. THE HILTON AREA

Trailheads: Rock Creek Lake and Old Highway 395
Distance: Approx. 13 miles
Difficulty: Class 2
Maps: Mt. Morgan, Mt. Abbot, Convict Lake 7.5 minute

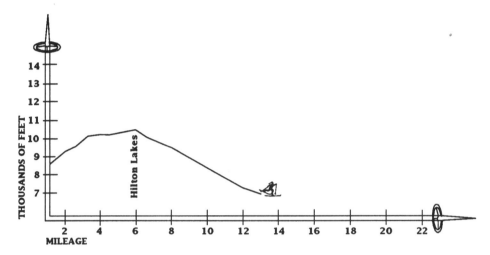

This shuttle tour is a perfect introduction to backcountry touring, and can be used as an early-season "shakedown" for a longer spring tour. It's mostly downhill, and visits the beautiful Hilton Lakes Basin before heading down Hilton Creek to the old road. Hilton Lakes also is a great base camp, with excellent bowl skiing in the cirques above the lakes and in Patricia Bowl, which is passed along the way. Pointless Peak, above Rock Creek Lake, also is one of the finest ski peaks in the range. Note: This canyon, like its neighbors, runs north- south, even though it's on the "east" side of the range.

DESCRIPTION

In early season, the Rock Creek road is plowed only to the gate at 8,900 feet. You can reach the Hilton Bench directly from the gate by climbing up the steep slope above the water tower. However, it's easier to take the road up to Rock Creek Lake (9,700 ft.). The moraine bench below the challenging east gullies of Pointless Peak (12,256 ft.) is followed north past the hidden cirque of Patricia Bowl (10,400 ft.). This cirque is surprisingly alpine in character and offers some of the best powder skiing in the Sierra in a spectacular setting.

Once on the Hilton Bench, the route circles very gently below the obvious avalanche slopes of Peak 11,950 to upper Hilton Lakes (10,350 ft.). There are a wide variety of skiing options from a base camp here, with Mt. Stanford (12,838 ft.) to the west providing both a great view and an excellent run back to camp.

A gentle run north through the trees takes you past the largest Hilton Lake (9,850 ft.) and on to Davis Lake (9,800 ft.). Directly to the west is a fine couloir leading down from the summit of Mt. Morgan North (13,005 ft.). The ski down the canyon follows the old mining road below the colorful cliffs and chutes of the Nevahbe Ridge, before reaching old Highway 395 at the Crowley Lake Campground (7,000 ft.).

Cutting up the powder in Patricia Bowl.   Photo: John Moynier

A windy day on the Hilton Bench.

Photo: Dion Goldsworthy

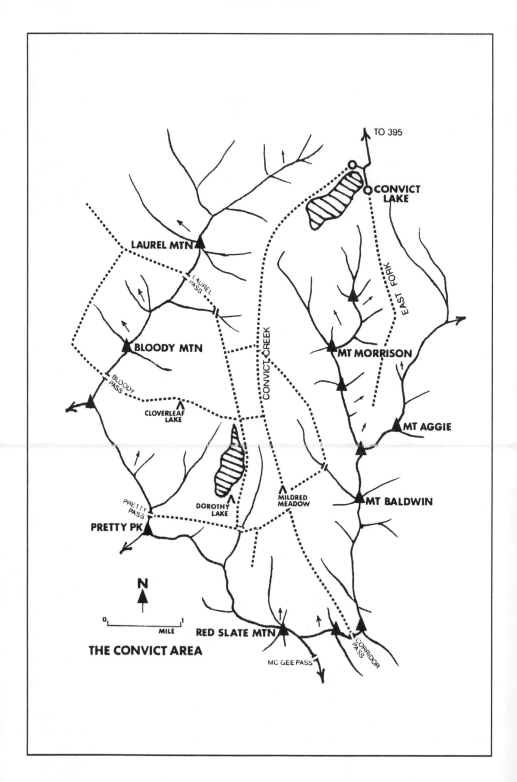

TO 395

CONVICT LAKE

LAUREL MTN

LAUREL PASS

EAST FORK

BLOODY MTN

CONVICT CREEK

MT MORRISON

BLOODY PASS

CLOVERLEAF LAKE

MT AGGIE

DOROTHY LAKE

MILDRED MEADOW

MT BALDWIN

PRETTY PASS

PRETTY PK

N

0 MILE 1

THE CONVICT AREA

RED SLATE MTN

CORRIDOR PASS

MC GEE PASS

12. THE CONVICT AREA

Trailhead: Convict Lake
Distance: Approx. 14 miles
Difficulty: Class 2
Maps: Bloody Mtn., Convict Lake 7.5 minute

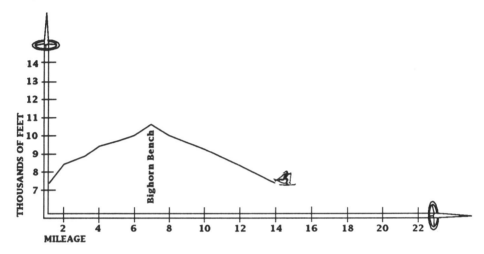

Convict Canyon is one of the most unique in the Sierra. The very colorful, folded cliffs of Mt. Morrison, Laurel Mountain and Mt. Baldwin are composed of the oldest rock in the range. These metamorphosed shales and limestones provide an interesting contrast to the prevalent greys and oranges of Sierra granite. There are many wonderful bowls and peaks to ski, including the north couloir of Red Slate Mountain. The side canyon carved by the east fork of Convict Creek makes a great tour, as does a longer connection with Mammoth, McGee or Rock Creek canyons. Note: Like the previous canyons, Convict Canyon runs north-south, even though it's on the "east" side of the range.

A view of Mt. Morrison and the east fork of Convict Creek.   Photo: John Moynier

DESCRIPTION

The tour begins at Convict Lake (7,600 ft.) and follows the summer trail past the great avalanche slopes of the Sevehah Cliffs and Laurel Mountain. Entering the mouth of the canyon, you pass a very interesting hidden couloir to the west, before reaching a ghost forest on the canyon floor. Follow the creek through a narrow cleft past the twisted remains of an avalanche-damaged bridge (9,000 ft.). Sinister black towers guard the entrance to the canyon, looking like something out of Tolkien. The canyon is very claustrophobic for a ways, before suddenly opening up at Mildred Lake (9,800 ft.).

The meadows at the south end make a fine place for a base camp as does Constance Lake (10,800 ft.). The bowls below Red Slate Mountain and Corridor Pass are accessed easily from here, and you have a great view back down the canyon. You can continue along the base of Mt. Baldwin to Bright Dot Lake (10,500 ft.), before dropping down the steep gully back to the bridge.

An alternate route is to ski up onto the bench to the west, which holds the huge Dorothy Lake (10,300 ft.), and then back down a steep gully to Mildred Lake. The run down Convict Creek is like a huge skateboard half-pipe – it's worth the trip just for this run.

Skiing below Red Slate Mountain.

Photo: John Moynier

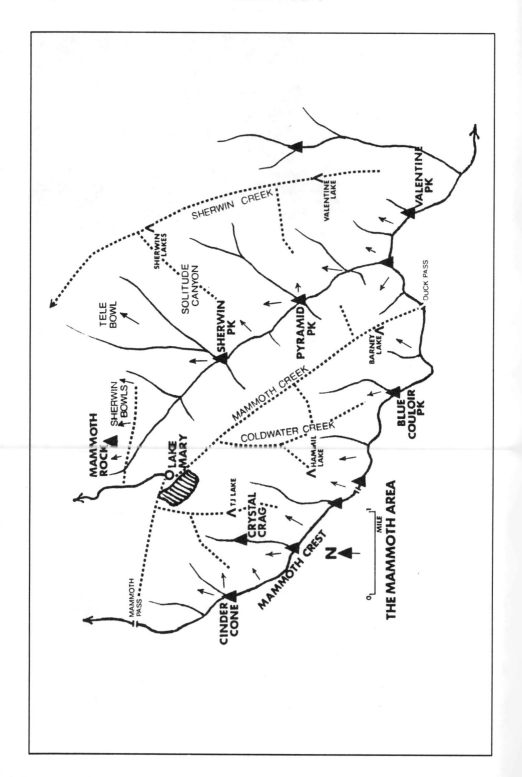

13. THE MAMMOTH AREA

Trailhead: Tamarack Lodge
Distance: Day Trips
Difficulty: Class 2-4
Maps: Bloody Mtn., Crystal Crag 7.5 minute

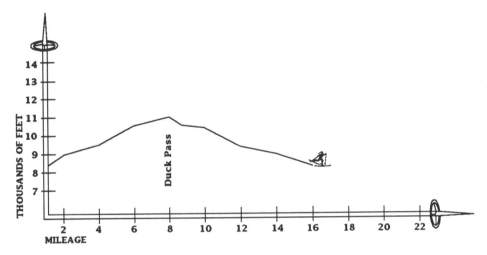

The prime attraction of the Mammoth area is its wonderful backcountry skiing opportunities. Challenging runs like the "Para Chute" and the Bloody Couloir are quite visible from U.S. Highway 395. The high bowls of the Mammoth Crest offer great winter powder skiing, as well as perfect spring corn well into the summer months.

The Sherwin bowls, right above the town of Mammoth, have long been home to local powder hounds. These great runs are extremely accessible. This area is threatened by potential development of a new ski area, though, and backcountry skiers could lose access to this wonderful haven.

Photo: John Moynier

A view of the Sherwin Bowls from Rock Chute (l) to the Rock (r).

Looking down at the fine turns in the Bloody Couloir.   Photo: Jim Stimson

DESCRIPTION

To backcountry skiers, Mammoth is like a candy store. The obvious couloir splitting the face of the dark red peak near the junction of State Highway 203 and U.S. Highway 395 is the Bloody Couloir on Bloody Mountain (12,600 ft.). The first of the Sherwin bowls is "Lost Bowl," located above Lost Lake (9,000 ft.). This is reached either by a long hike up the Valentine Lake trail, or by climbing onto the ridge from the Mammoth Creek side. The rocky peak to the right is known as Pyramid Peak (1,800 ft.) which is the apex of the Sherwin triangle. Splitting these cliffs is a very steep couloir known as the "Para Chute."

Closer to town, the valley above Sherwin Lakes is known as Solitude Canyon. These wonderful tree runs are targeted to be completely changed by the ski area development. At the foot of the ridge above the Sierra Meadows Touring Center is the Tele Bowl. This quite steep slope is visible from town and often gets just one pair of tracks after a storm. Another fine tree run lies just above.

The runs of the main Sherwin ridge are most easily accessed from Tamarack Lodge (8,700 ft.): By leaving a car at the golf course at the base (8,000 ft.), you can make this a shuttle. Ski up the road (staying out of the groomed tracks) to the Mammoth Pack Station. From there, follow the old mine road to the base of the cliffs on the ridge. A short chute leads through the cliffs and onto the broad plateau (10,100 ft.) at the top. From there, ski out the plateau until you reach the top of your desired descent. Most of these runs congregate at the bottom of the avalanche slope near the lone tree that was spared. Beware of the very avalanche-prone bowl next to the Rock.

Skiing the main avalanche path of the Sherwin Bowls.   Photo: Andy Selters

Looking up from the town of Mammoth, the rocky cliffs high on the left harbor the Rock Chute. Immediately to the right are the Fingers, which also are quite steep near the top. The obvious avalanche path in the center is a result of the February 1986 storm cycle, and provides the easiest and most straightforward descent. In the trees to the right is the "Hose," which usually is the first line to be skied after a storm. Finally, Easter Bowl lies directly above the prominent Mammoth Rock, and provides the easiest return to a car left at Tamarack. All of these runs obviously are exposed to very high avalanche hazard.

From the top of Mammoth Mountain, the runs of the Mammoth Crest above the Mammoth Lakes are very prominent. From the low saddle of Mammoth Pass (9,300 ft.) the runs range south along the crest. Hollywood Bowl and the Cinder Cone (10,400 ft.) are located just above Lake George (9,000 ft.). The massive cornice above the Crystal Crag bowl is called "Jaws." The moderate bowl just above TJ Lake (9,250 ft.) is known as "Child's Play." Above it, and left on the crest, is the "Ship's Prow" and the associated nautically-named couloirs.

Along the Mammoth Crest (11,200 ft.), there are numerous bowls and chutes above the scenic Hammil Lake (10,000 ft.). These are best accessed via Coldwater Creek. Farther south and east along the crest lies the popular Blue Couloir, and the bowls above Barney Lake (10,250 ft.). These can be reached either by Coldwater or Mammoth Creeks. Finally, Duck Pass (10,800 ft.) is a popular day-tour destination, especially when followed by the great run back along the Mammoth Creek to Lake Mary (8,900 ft.) and Tamarack Lodge (8,700 ft.).

A view of the Mammoth Crest above Mammoth Lakes.   Photo: John Moynier

Enjoying the fine Sierra sun and skiing.

Photo: John Moynier

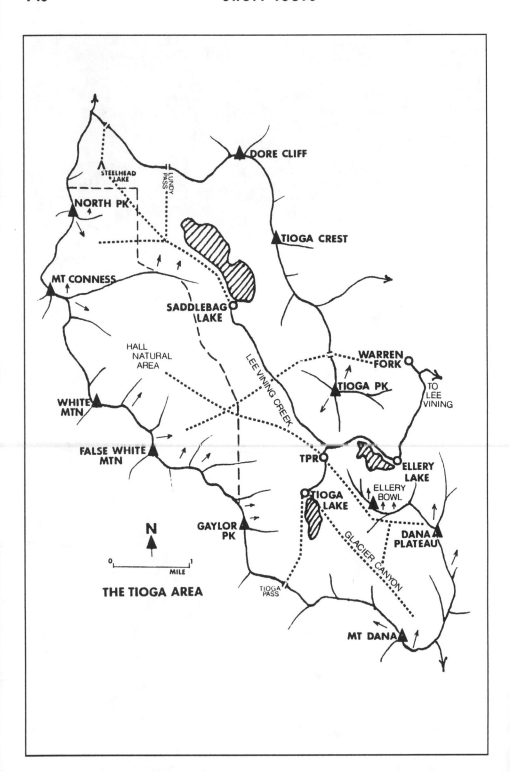

THE TIOGA AREA

14. THE TIOGA AREA

Trailhead: Tioga Pass Resort
Distance: Day Tours
Difficulty: Class 2-4
Maps: Tioga Pass, Mt. Dana 7.5 minute

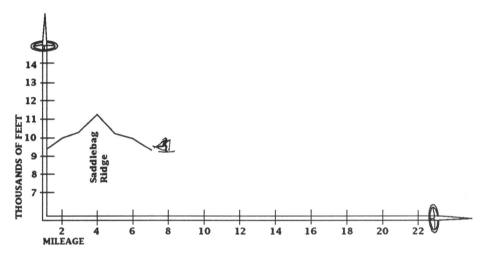

In early springtime, a great thing happens. Before they open State Highway 120 all the way through Yosemite Park, they clear the road for fishermen to the Tioga Pass Resort (TPR). Driving up the Tioga Pass road from Lee Vining, you are impressed immediately by the great bowl and couloirs above Ellery Lake. Hidden above this is the Dana Couloir, below the summit of Mt. Dana. As you round the corner, however, your eye is drawn across the lake to a great white bowl on the crest. These fine peaks are right on the border of Yosemite National Park.

Skiing down "False White" Mountain.   Photo: Dave Page

DESCRIPTION

The first runs north of Tioga Pass (9,945 ft.) are off Gaylor Peak (11,000 ft.). These runs are quite steep, but due to their proximity to the road, they can be skied over and over again. Directly behind the Tioga Pass Resort (9,550 ft.) is the great bowl of False White Mountain (12,000 ft.). It's called this because it frequently is confused with the real White Mountain (12,000 ft.) one mile to the northwest.

False White can be accessed from Gaylor Peak, TPR or the Saddlebag road at Sawmill Campground. The Gaylor approach follows the crest west to the summit. The TPR route ascends past the ruins of the historic mining town of Bennettville and onto Fantail Lake (9,950 ft.). The Fantail Gullies lie just above. The route from Sawmill meets the TPR route at Spuller Lake (10,300 ft.), then climbs a broad gully to the south and accesses the bowl below the north summit. This approach, while longer, often offers better skiing conditions later in the year. White Mountain and Mt. Conness (12,590 ft.) also have good runs above Carnegie Station, and are reached from Sawmill Campground.

The best place for bowl skiing in this area is the ridge (11,200 ft.) just west of Saddlebag Lake (10,100 ft.). There are a wide variety of slopes and gullies along the ridge as it stretches towards Mt. Conness. Further to the north are the runs off North Peak (12,242 ft.). The southeast face offers a fairly moderate run, while the north couloirs present very steep and challenging descents. Finally, Tioga Peak (11,513 ft.) offers fine runs on its south side in early season, and on its north side later in the year.

Photo: John Moynier

A view of the bowls above Saddlebag Lake.

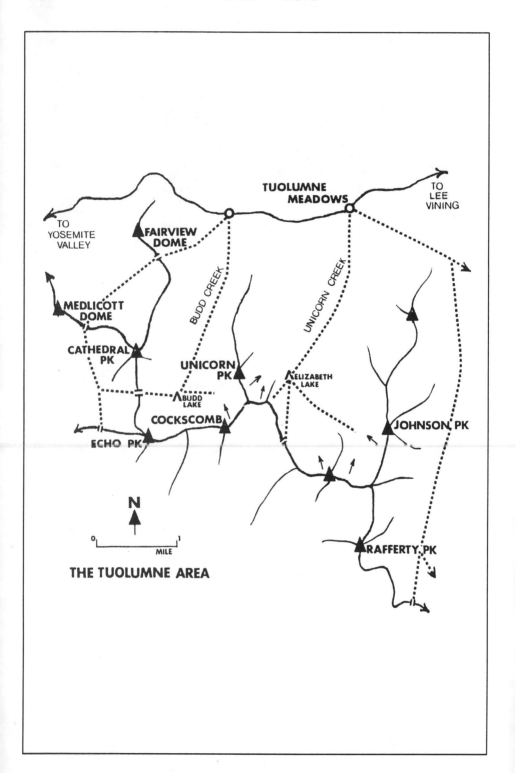

THE TUOLUMNE AREA

15. THE TUOLUMNE AREA

Trailhead: Tuolumne Meadows
Distance: Approx. 10 miles (22 miles from Tioga Pass Resort)
Difficulty: Class 2
Maps: Tenaya Lake, Vogelsang Peak 7.5 minute

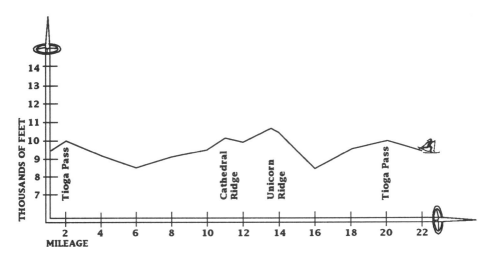

Generally, the Tioga Pass road does not open into Yosemite National Park until mid-May or later. There usually is fine skiing in the Elizabeth Lake bowls below Unicorn Peak at this time of year. However, the best time to visit Tuolumne is before the road opens. There is a stone shelter available to skiers, and there are rangers on duty all winter. At this time, there are unlimited numbers of wonderful ski tours amongst the spectacular domes and spires. Not to be missed is an early-spring descent of the south slopes of Mt. Hoffmann and the run off Mammoth Peak to the east of the meadows.

A view of the spectacular Cockscomb Bowl.   Photo: Dave Page

DESCRIPTION

Follow the Tioga Pass Road to the winter shelter at Tuolumne Meadows (8,600 ft.). Ski down the road to the trailhead for the Cathedral Lakes, just east of Fairview Dome. Follow the general course of the Muir Trail as it climbs through the trees and onto the forested plateau (9,500 ft.) west of the inspiring tower of Cathedral Peak, before traversing around to upper Cathedral Lake (9,600 ft.). From here, head up the slope toward the sheer south face of the peak, then head over the very broad saddle (10,150 ft.) to a base camp at Budd Lake (9,975 ft.). From here, a short climb to the east takes you to the great bowl below the rocky Cockscomb (11,065 ft.).

Most folks ski out the way they came, or via the Budd Creek drainage, but it's also possible to cross the ridge south of Unicorn Peak (10,700 ft.), and ski down the Elizabeth Lake Bowl and back to Tuolumne.

Enjoying the winter sun below Feather Peak.   Photo: Vern Clevenger

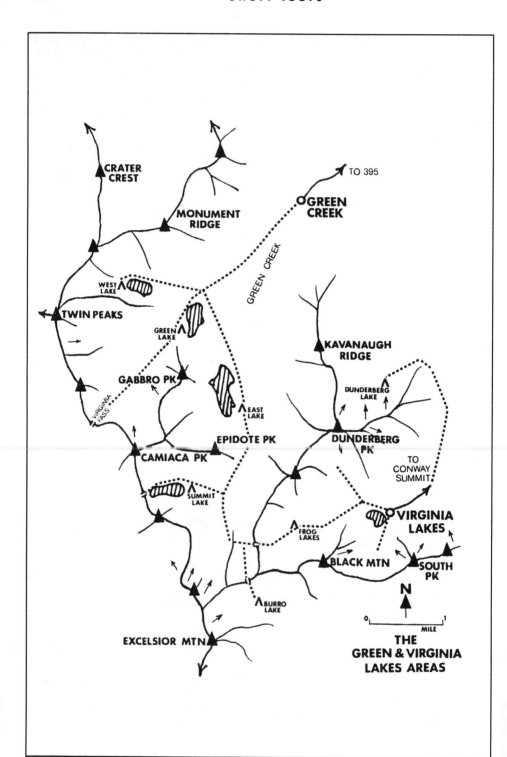

THE
GREEN & VIRGINIA
LAKES AREAS

16. THE GREEN CREEK AND VIRGINIA LAKES AREA

Trailheads: Virginia Lakes and Green Creek
Distance: Approx. 21 miles
Difficulty: Class 2-3
Maps: Dunderberg Peak 7.5 minute

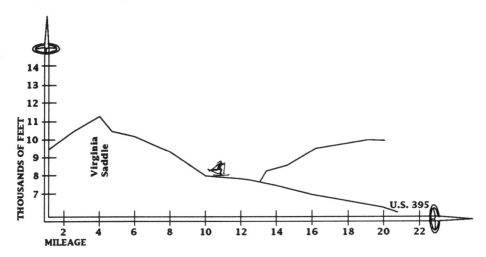

The Virginia Lakes area is one of the finest base camps for bowl skiing in the High Sierra. Mt. Olsen, South Peak, Black Mountain and Dunderberg Peak all offer great and varied descents. This tour also is highly recommendable as one of the best "one pass" introductory tours in the range. It starts at a very high trailhead and skis over a fairly low pass before making a long and enjoyable descent down Green Creek.

Skiing off the shoulder of Mt. Olsen.   Photo: John Moynier

DESCRIPTION

The tour begins at Virginia Lakes (9,700 ft.), below the impressive gullies of Dunderberg Peak (12,374 ft.). To the south are the excellent bowls of Mt. Olsen (11,086 ft.), South Peak (11,300 ft.) and Black Mountain (11,797 ft.), all of which loom above the lakes. Follow the drainage up past Blue Lake (9,900 ft.) and on to Frog Lakes (10,375 ft.), where the general course of the summer trail is taken to the low saddle (11,150 ft.) to the west. The summit of Excelsior Mountain (12,446 ft.) is reached easily on skis from the pass.

From below the pass, it's possible to look across into the hanging valley of Summit Lake. A wonderful descent takes you north to Hoover Lakes (9,800 ft.) on the floor of the glacial canyon of upper Green Creek. From the lakes, a steady descent follows the summer trail past Gilman Lake (9,500 ft.) and down to the large East Lake (9,450 ft.). From the lake, you can follow either the east or west forks of Green Creek as they descend through the forest to the road at Green Creek Campground (8,000 ft.).

If it's still early in the season, you may be able to ski down the road almost to U.S. Highway 395 (6,650 ft.). More likely, however, you'll want to climb east out of Green Creek canyon after a couple of miles, to the Dunderberg road at Sinnamon Meadow (8,400 ft.), and return to Virginia Lakes from there. A fine base camp also can be placed off this road at Dunderberg Lake, just below the wonderful bowls on the north side of Dunderberg Peak.

A view of South Peak and Black Mountain.

Photo: John Moynier

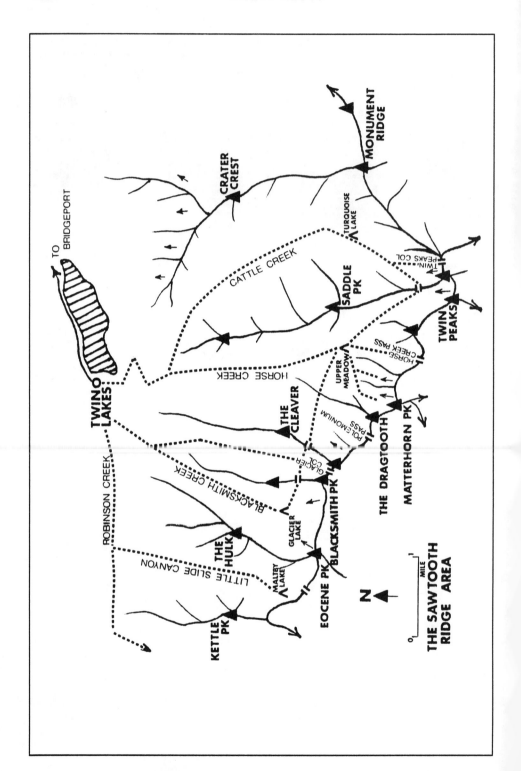

TWIN LAKES

TO BRIDGEPORT

CRATER CREST

MONUMENT RIDGE

TURQUOISE LAKE

CATTLE CREEK

SADDLE PK

TWIN PEAKS COL

TWIN PEAKS

HORSE CREEK PASS

HORSE CREEK

UPPER MEADOW

THE CLEAVER

POLEMONIUM PASS

MATTERHORN PK

THE DRAGTOOTH

GLACIER COL

BLACKSMITH CREEK

GLACIER LAKE

ROBINSON CREEK

BLACKSMITH PK

THE HULK

EOCENE PK

MALIBU LAKE

LITTLE SLIDE CANYON

KETTLE PK

N

THE SAWTOOTH RIDGE AREA

0   MILE   1

17. THE SAWTOOTH RIDGE AREA

Trailhead: Twin Lakes
Distance: Approx.13 miles
Difficulty: Class 3-4
Maps: Matterhorn Peak, Dunderberg Peak, Buckeye Ridge 7.5 minute

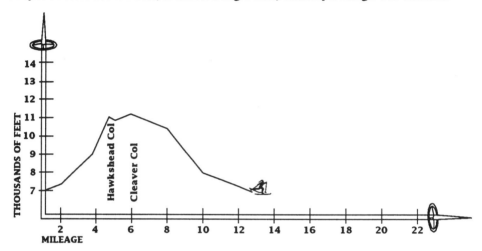

This route tours the glaciers on the north side of the Sawtooth Ridge. This really is a mountaineering course, linking a series of extremely fine ski bowls. The ragged granite towers of the ridge provide a spectacular backdrop, with the grand finale at Matterhorn Peak and the fantastic run down Horse Creek. This certainly is not a tour for everyone – but for the ski mountaineer who wants to combine some great climbing with some great skiing, Sawtooth Ridge is the place to be.

An easier tour follows the Cattle Creek drainage up past Turquoise Lake and onto the glacier below the imposing north couloirs of Twin Peaks. A short traverse takes you over the low saddle to the west, and on down the great natural half pipe of upper Horse Creek to the meadow below.

DESCRIPTION

The route begins at Twin Lakes (7,100 ft.) and follows Blacksmith Creek as it climbs steeply out of the Robinson Creek canyon. At the fork in the creek above the falls (8,100 ft.), head up the main drainage, below the great east tower of the "Incredible Hulk" (11,581 ft.). Continue climbing until you reach Glacier Lake (10,050 ft.), at the head of the cirque. To the southwest, the large bowl below Eocene Peak (11,581 ft.) offers great skiing.

To continue the tour, climb up to the narrow notch in the ridge to the southwest (10,800 ft.), just below the sharp arête of Blacksmith Peak. A high contouring traverse at the base of this sheer face takes you below Glacier Col, across the Cleaver at Cleaver Notch (10,900 ft.), and to the glacier right below the main part of the Sawtooth Ridge.

If you are trying to climb Matterhorn Peak, circle along the base of the glacier until it's possible to skirt below the great cliff of the "Dragtooth." Climb up onto the Matterhorn Peak glacier (11,400 ft.) until you are at the foot of the east couloir.

Otherwise, follow the creek down a great run down to the Horse Creek Meadow (8,300 ft.). This also is a great place for a spring base camp, as you can also easily access the gullies of Twin Peaks (12,300 ft.). You can make this tour even longer by skiing down Cattle Creek.

The Sawtooth Ridge as seen from Bridgeport. Photo: John Moynier

Skiing Matterhorn Peak.

Photo: Dave Page

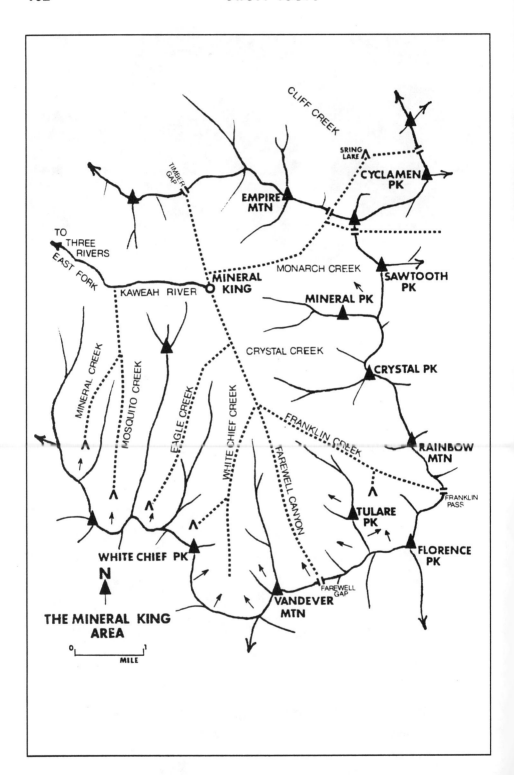

THE MINERAL KING
AREA

N

18. THE MINERAL KING AREA

Trailhead: Mineral King
Distance: Approx. 18 miles
Difficulty: Class 2-3
Maps: Mineral King 7.5 minute

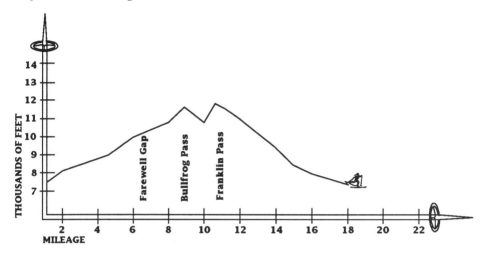

The Mineral King valley is unique not only to the west side, but to the Sierra in general. Just getting into it in winter and early spring can be a major undertaking. The road may be clear as far as Silver City, six miles west of the valley proper. Once you're in the valley, the goal is to get into the high bowls lying above.

Touring in Mineral King usually means leaving the valley floor (7,700 ft.). The routes into the canyons are quite straightforward. In general, you'll want to ski west-facing bowls early in the day, before the sun softens them too much. Base camps at the head of White Chief Bowl, Farewell Canyon and the Franklin Lakes are the most popular, with numerous peak descents and short tours possible.

There are fine tours into high base camps above the valley, notably in the Mineral Lakes and Mosquito Lakes cirques. The best option, however, may be to base yourself in the valley itself and just do day tours into these high cirques. Note: The entire area is exposed to great avalanche hazard in both winter and spring.

A view of Mineral King Valley.

Photo: Vern Clevenger

DESCRIPTION

Perhaps the finest loop trip from the Mineral King valley is the Farewell Gap to Franklin Pass tour. From the valley floor (7,700 ft.), follow the summer dirt road south into Farewell Canyon, which climbs gently to Crystal Creek (7,950 ft.). Continue up the canyon past the junction of Crystal and Franklin Creeks, then on up the bowl to Farewall Gap.

From the pass, there are fine views to the south. Traverse east across steep slopes to Bullfrog Lakes (11,000 ft.). Bullfrog Pass (11,600 ft.) is the low point on the steep headwall to the east. After crossing the pass, drop down to the small lake below (10,900 ft.), and follow its outlet creek north to the head of Rattlesnake Canyon (10,500 ft.).

The route then follows the summer trail as it climbs north and east to Franklin Pass (11,700 ft.). From the pass, drop into the bowl, then continue to the largest of Franklin Lakes (10,350 ft.) before following the creek steeply down to Farewell Canyon and out to Mineral King.

Skiing near Black Rock Pass.

Photo: John Dittli

Shussing in late-spring powder.

Photo: John Moynier

CLASSIC PEAK DESCENTS

THE SIERRA NEVADA FAULT has worked to create an enormous escarpment on the east side of the range. Along this escarpment, there are an infinite number of wonderful ski descents. How do you pick which are the classics? Well, it seems whenever groups of backcountry skiers get together, the same names always pop up: Elderberry Canyon, Basin Mountain, Mt. Wood, Birch Mountain.

I suppose I should round these out to a "Top 20" of classic descents. The three peaks I would add certainly are classic descents, maybe even the best. Perhaps they should be kept "secret," but here they are anyway: Mt. Langley (14,027 ft.) via Tuttle Creek (with its 6,000-foot descent), Vagabond Peak (13,374 ft., with a 4,000-foot drop down to Parchers Lodge), and Mt. Locke's (12,634 ft.) Wahoo Gullies, my personal choice for the finest ski descent in the range. What are your favorites? Maybe you'd rather just keep them a secret.

One thing all these peaks have in common is long descents. Opportunities for 6,000 vertical feet or more are possible. I should note, however, that when there is skiing to the base of these giants, it's almost assured that it won't be great top to bottom. However, there will be variety – it may be that you'll ski powder near the top, choice windboard on an exposed ridge, power a couple of turns through breakable crust and then descend thousands of feet of velvety corn down into the sagebrush below.

These peaks are mini-expeditions by themselves. Six thousand feet down generally means the same up, and that's a big day in anyone's book. Make sure you get an early start and remember: timing is everything. There may only be a few days when all the conditions are right, making the peaks worth the effort. Anyone of these would be a skier's dream, to do all of them is a lifetime goal.

1. Mt. Williamson

Route: North Fork of Bair's Creek
Trailhead: Foothill Road
Vertical: Approx. 5,500 feet
Difficulty: Class 3-4
Maps: Mt. Williamson, Manzanar 7.5 minute

Description

The route itself is quite obvious from U.S. Highway 395. Getting to it, however, requires a bit of routefinding. First, take the Onion Valley road west from Independence to its junction with the Foothill Road. This rough dirt road leads south past the turnoff to the Shepherds Pass trailhead, crosses Shepherds Creek, and climbs up to the very base of the mountain at the North Fork of Bairs Creek (6,400 ft.). An alternate approach can be made from the Manzanar historic monument by heading west on one of the maze of dirt roads, and hoping the one you picked reaches the Foothill road.

To reach the enticing ski slopes above, you first must pass through the tangled brush of the steep lower canyon. It's questionable which is the lesser of two evils: carrying your skis in your hands or strapping them on your pack. Either method is bound to bring grief. At about 9,000 feet, the canyon finally becomes a ski route, as you head up into the monstrous cirque perched on the side of the peak.

The massive headwall at the top of the cirque (12,550 ft.) can be passed on the right, but if you intend to ski the central couloir, you should ascend that route. At the top of the headwall (13,200 ft.), broad slopes lead to the summit plateau and the top (14,375 ft.) of California' second highest peak.

The descent route returns the way you came. If the headwall is too steep, you can ski down the more moderate slopes of Bairs Creek to the south before circling back into the North Fork.

Mt. Williamson.   Photo: John Moynier

2. KEARSARGE PEAK

Route: Sardine Canyon
Trailhead: Onion Valley
Vertical: Approx. 5,000 feet
Difficulty: Class 2-3
Maps: Kearsarge Peak 7.5 minute

DESCRIPTION

This adventure starts at Onion Valley (9,200 ft.). Begin by climbing alongside the outlet stream of the Golden Trout Lakes. At the junction of the two forks (10,900 ft.), follow a steep gully on the northeast to the summit ridge (12,100 ft.). The very gentle bowl leading down past Sardine Lake (11,550 ft.) begins here. By continuing on to the summit (12,600 ft.), you can get to the great northeast gullies that drop steeply into Sardine Canyon.

Either way, continue down the wonderful canyon bottom until you reach a mining road (7,200 ft.) that takes you back to the Onion Valley road. By arranging a car or bike shuttle, it is possible to get an extra 2,000-foot descent below the start. The disadvantage of this is that because you've ascending a different route, you won't know what conditions will be like on the descent.

Kearsarge Peak.

Photo: John Moynier

3. MT. PERKINS

Route: Armstrong and Spook Canyons
Trailhead: Sawmill Creek
Vertical: Approx. 5,500 feet
Difficulty: Class 2-3 and Class 3-4
Maps: Aberdeen 7.5 minute

DESCRIPTION

Armstrong Canyon is a very long, but wonderfully moderate descent. Spook Canyon and the gully just to its north provide more difficult challenges for the expert skier. These gullies lie to the east of the crest in the vicinity of Mt. Perkins. To reach them, take the Division Creek road past the powerhouse, then the Sawmill Pass Trail, before ascending to Scotty Springs (6,000 ft.). A mining road leads up to the north onto the ridge from here.

Armstrong Canyon is the moderate valley that reaches toward the crest from the Rudy Mine (8,400 ft.). It is possible to ascend this canyon all the way to the Sierra Crest. A steep headwall reaches the crest just south of the summit of Mt. Perkins (12,600 ft.). The fine run down the canyon brings you into the high desert and a traverse back around to the car.

The peaklet (11,765 ft.) above Scotty Springs can be reached via the shallow gully to the north. The ascent gully usually provides the best descent, but Spook Canyon also can provide an extremely steep and narrow drop straight to the car below.

Photo: John Moynier

Mt. Perkins.

4. BIRCH MOUNTAIN

Route: Tinemaha Creek
Trailhead: McMurray Meadows
Vertical: Approx. 6,000 feet
Difficulty: Class 3
Maps: Split Mtn., Fish Springs 7.5 minute

DESCRIPTION

Like Mt. Williamson to the south, finding the route to the bottom of this giant is more difficult than the route itself. Leave the Big Pine Creek road a few miles west of town, and take the long dirt road to Mc Murray Meadows. At the south end of the meadows, a trail leads up the mountain to Tinemaha Creek. Follow the creek drainage west toward the huge cirque below Mt. Bolton Brown. Then, follow the southeast slopes to the summit of Birch Mountain (13,665 ft.). There is a great view of the Palisades from here. Retrace the route for the descent.

Birch Mountain.

Photo: John Moynier

5. BASIN MOUNTAIN

Route: Basin Couloir
Trailhead: Buttermilk Road
Vertical: Approx. 5,000 feet
Difficulty: Class 3
Maps: Mt. Tom, Tungsten Hills 7.5 minute

DESCRIPTION

The east couloir on Basin Mountain is one of the premier ski descents in the range. This very long, aesthetic route is plainly visible from Bishop, and offers great skiing. To reach the base, drive State Highway 168 west from Bishop, then take the dirt Buttermilk road past the boulders and on to the trailhead for the Horton Lakes (8,000 ft.). You may choose to follow the old mining road into the massive basin midway up the peak, or climb the lower slopes directly to the couloir.

The couloir itself is very broad and surprisingly moderate. At the col (13,000 ft.) you may wish to leave your skis and climb around to the west ridge and the summit (13,240). In good years, it is possible to ski from the col almost all of the way back to the car.

Basin Mountain.   Photo: John Moynier

6. Mt. Tom

Route: *Elderberry Canyon*
Trailhead: *Rovanna*
Vertical: *Approx. 5,000 feet*
Difficulty: *Class 3*
Maps: *Mt. Tom, Mt. Morgan 7.5 minute*

DESCRIPTION

This simply is the finest peak descent in the Sierra. The sweeping line of Elderberry Canyon leading down from the summit of Mt. Tom is a memorable sight to anyone driving south toward Bishop on U.S. Highway 395. The mountain is reached via the Pine Creek road at the small mining town of Rovanna. A dirt road leads to the base (6,300 ft.), where an old mining trail climbs into the canyon. The route climbs up over steeper bumps and flats to the Lambert Mine (10,850 ft.), which lies in the monstrous cirque at the head of the canyon.

It is possible to climb up the steep headwall (12,350 ft.) to the west, and on to the summit (13,652 ft.) via the north ridge. This headwall provides the most challenging skiing on the route. Most folks, however, turn back somewhere above 11,200 feet and enjoy the long descent to the car before the snow gets too soft.

Photo: John Moynier

Mt. Tom.

7. Mt. Morgan South

Route: Francis Gullies
Trailhead: Rock Creek
Vertical: Approx. 4,800 feet
Difficulty: Class 2-3
Maps: Mt. Morgan 7.5 minute

Description

Mt. Morgan is one of the easiest big peaks to ski in the Sierra, and has one of the finest views. This peak also is one of the better ones to attempt in mid-winter. From the trailhead at Rock Creek (8,900 ft.), ski up the road to Rock Creek Lake (9,700 ft.). Follow the marked ski trail east onto the plateau of the East Fork of Rock Creek (10,200 ft.) and climb up the drainage to Kenneth Lake (10,400 ft.) before circling south up the steep slopes to an open bench above Francis Lake (11,000 ft.). Follow this natural ski trail toward the obvious gullies, then climb onto the north shoulder (12,500 ft.). From here, climb to the summit of Mt. Morgan (13,748 ft.).

The steep north-facing gullies provide a very challenging descent. In winter, the steep forested slopes above Kenneth Lake offer some of the finest powder skiing on the east side. From the bench, a number of fine powder gullies drop down to the meadow at Rock Creek Lodge (9,400 ft.), and a marked ski trail follows the creek through the woods back to the car.

Photo: John Moynier

Mt. Morgan.

8. Mt. Morgan North

Route: Esha Canyon
Trailhead: McGee Creek
Vertical: Approx. 5,000 feet
Difficulty: Class 3
Maps: Convict Lake 7.5 minute

Description

This has long been a local favorite, as it provides a great descent down a wonderful, hidden canyon close to the access road. From just below the McGee Creek Pack Station (7,700 ft.), climb up into the hanging valley to the south. Esha Canyon is protected from view by the very colorful Nevahbe Ridge. The ascent follows a series of steep benches and flat meadows to the head of the north-facing cirque.

From here, a moderately steep slope heads up and left to the huge plateau just below the summit (13,005 ft.). Steeper descents can be found down the north slope of the Nevahbe Ridge, as well as down one of the east gullies to Hilton Creek. Another popular descent takes one of the very steep gullies on the northeast face of the pyramidal peak that looms over the canyon.

Skiing below Bear Creek Spire.

Photo: John Moynier

9. Mᴛ. McGᴇᴇ

Route: 395 Gullies
Trailhead: Highway 395
Vertical: Approx. 4,000 feet
Difficulty: Class 3
Maps: Convict Lake 7.5 minute

Dᴇsᴄʀɪᴘᴛɪᴏɴ

Mt. McGee (10,900 ft.) was the site of one of the first ski areas in the eastern Sierra. The rope-tow operation situated at the base of these gullies eventually was moved to the now mega-developed Mammoth Mountain. Mammoth Heli-Ski also used to visit Mt. McGee. These gullies still are very popular, and provide a classic "roadside attraction" above U.S. Highway 395 (6,900 ft.) near Crowley Lake. The central, northeast-facing gullies are the most popular, but there are very skiable runs down the northwest and southeast sides as well.

Mt. McGee and Esha Canyon.

Photo: John Moynier

10. BLOODY MOUNTAIN

Route: Bloody Couloir
Trailhead: Laurel Lakes Road
Vertical: Approx. 4,000 feet
Difficulty: Class 4
Maps: Bloody Mtn. 7.5 minute

DESCRIPTION

Driving into the town of Mammoth Lakes, the dark slot of the Bloody Couloir looms ominously above the road. This is probably the premier local "extreme" ski descent, and is skied quite often. To reach the base of the couloir, follow the four-wheel drive road from near the YMCA camp (7,500 ft.) to the shady meadow (8,800 ft.) below the Laurel Lakes. From here, ski up the road above the Laurel Lakes, and around to the open slope at the base of the couloir.

There are many options from here. The Y-shaped gullies to the left offer very steep skiing, and are reached from below or the large snowfield to the left of the summit. The main couloir is split by two prominent rock towers. The best ascent route is along the left side of the towers, and also provides the best fall-line descent. The main Bloody Couloir drops very steeply from the summit (12,544 ft.) on the west side of the high tower before joining the other route above the lower tower. The gully dropping down the west side of the lower tower also offers good skiing.

Bloody Mountain.

Photo: John Moynier

11. MT. RITTER

Route: Ediza Couloir
Trailhead: Agnew Meadows
Vertical: Approx. 4,000 feet
Difficulty: Class 3-4
Maps: Mt. Ritter 7.5 minute

DESCRIPTION

Mt. Ritter is a very popular ski peak in spring, and can be reached in a day after the Devil's Postpile road opens. From the Agnew Meadows Campground (8,600 ft.), follow the summer trail down to the bridge on the Middle Fork of the San Joaquin River (8,100 ft.) before climbing back up to Shadow Lake (8,700 ft.). From here, follow Shadow Creek up to Lake Ediza (9,250 ft.).

Follow the drainage to the west up to the small glacier on the south side of the peak. From here, a short gully leads to the summit slopes and the top (13,157 ft.). There is a tremendous view of the Minarets, as well as southern Yosemite National Park, from the top. The broad summit snowfield funnels down to the very steep couloir before regaining the open bowl back to Ediza Lake and the drainage leading to Shadow Lake.

Mt. Ritter.

Photo: John Moynier

12. CARSON PEAK

Route: Devil's Slide
Trailhead: June Lake Loop
Vertical: Approx. 3,500 feet
Difficulty: Class 3-4
Maps: Mammoth Mtn., June Lake 7.5 minute

DESCRIPTION

Carson Peak has long been a popular ski descent with the local skiers. In fact, there were a number of races held on this slope before World War II. The lower gully, known as the "Devil's Slide," is very prominent from the June Lake Loop near Silver Lake. The upper bowls are in plain sight from the slopes of June Mountain ski area. The tricky part is the connecting ledges between the two runs.

From the Fern Creek Trailhead (7,300 ft.), take the trail up until it's possible to make a short traverse into the gully. Follow the gully to its top (9,200 ft.), then weave your way above the cliffs into the steep upper bowl, and on to the summit (10,900 ft.). You should be able to ski almost all the way back to the car. The bowls above Fern Lake (8,900 ft.) also offer great skiing possibilities.

Carson Peak – Devil's Slide.

Photo: John Moynier

13. Mt. Wood

Route: East Gullies
Trailhead: Silver Lake
Vertical: Approx. 5,500 feet
Difficulty: Class 3
Maps: Koip Peak, June Lake 7.5 minute

Description

This is another of the great eastside giants, and these gullies dominate the view from U.S. Highway 395 north of the main June Lake junction. If you time it right, you can hike up the trail from Silver Lake (7,200 ft.), to the bench at 9,000 feet, and finish by skiing down to the road at Grant Lake (7,200 ft.) for a bonus 1,800 feet of descent. It also is possible to reach the bench from the Parker Lake trailhead (7,800 ft.) to the north.

From the bench, you have a choice of options. The most moderate descent takes the left-hand gully to the upper southeast slopes. The main gullies drop straight down from the summit (12,650 ft.) through the cliffs and back to the bench, offering the most aesthetic descent. Many folks, however, choose to enjoy a couple of runs on the great east slope below the cliffs (11,000 ft.), and don't bother to go to the summit. To ski down to Grant Lake, take the steep, aspen-filled gully just north of the dome (9,200 ft.) on the eastern edge of the bench.

Photo: John Moynier

Mt. Wood.

14. MT. GIBBS

Route: *Walker Gullies*
Trailhead: *Walker Lake*
Vertical: *Approx. 4,500 feet*
Difficulty: *Class 3-4*
Maps: *Mt. Dana 7.5 minute*

DESCRIPTION

Mt. Gibbs is a very interesting peak. The northeast summit (12,565 ft.) sits at the head of a great cirque. The run down the north glacier past Kidney Lake (10,400 ft.) and Gibbs Lake (9,500 ft.) to the Lee Vining Campground (7,400 ft.) is another of the giant (5,500 ft.) descents. Our route, however, takes the eastern gullies lying above Walker Lake (7,950 ft.), which is reached via a dirt road from the northern end of the June Lake Loop. These very steep avalanche gullies are quite similar to those on their neighbor, Mt. Wood, only steeper.

The main peak of Mt. Gibbs (12,773 ft.) also offers fine ski possibilities down its south slopes to the Sardine Lakes (9,900 ft.), as well as the north and west slopes leading to the Dana Fork of the Tuolumne River and the Tioga road at the Dana Meadows (9,600 ft.).

Mt. Gibbs.

Photo: John Moynier

15. Mt. Dana

Route: *Dana Couloir & Ellery Couloir*
Trailhead: *Tioga Pass and Ellery Lake*
Vertical: *Approx. 4,000 feet combined*
Difficulty: *Class 4*
Maps: *Mt. Dana 7.5 minute*

DESCRIPTION

This is a two-part springtime ritual. By starting at Tioga Pass and finishing at Ellery Lake, you get two great descents in one shot. The trip begins at the entrance to Yosemite National Park at Tioga Pass (9,945 ft.) and follows the trail up the northwest slopes of Mt. Dana to the summit (13,057 ft.). There is a tremendous view of Yosemite National Park from here, as well as a view down into Glacier Canyon and the Dana Couloir below. Mono Lake stretches out to the east beyond the Dana Plateau. At the north end of that plateau lies the Ellery Bowl, and the hidden Ellery Couloir.

To reach the Dana Couloir, ski down the south face to the saddle at the foot of the small peaklet. The broad couloir begins moderately, then steepens for an unrelieved 1,000-foot drop onto the glacier. At the glacier, the angle relents, and a fun run down Glacier Canyon takes you past Dana Lake (11,100 ft.) and onto the bench that climbs onto the Dana Plateau.

Of course, you can ski all the way out Glacier Canyon and circle around to the pass. An even more challenging alternative follows the "Solstice" gully on the north side of the peak, dropping straight down from the summit to Dana Lake. This is steep and narrow and often is guarded by a large cornice at the top.

At the north end of the Dana plateau (11,500 ft.), there is a large saddle with a cornice barring the upper reaches of Ellery Bowl. Further to the west, the very narrow entrance to the Ellery Couloir also often is filled by a cornice. This extremely steep gully is very popular as a descent in itself, and exits the very center of the main cliff above the bowl. There also are a series of other enjoyable chutes dropping off the rim to the west. Once in the Ellery Bowl, an extremely fine descent brings you to the dam at Ellery Lake (9,500 ft.). The spring skiing is so good here that many folks choose to forego Mt. Dana and just ski the bowl and these chutes.

On the east side of the plateau (11,600 ft.) are some of the wildest ski descents in the Sierra. A series of extremely steep chutes drop between towering granite pillars and into two great glacial cirques. These lead through some very rugged terrain all the way down to Lee Vining Campground (7,400 ft.).

Mt. Dana and Ellery Gullies.

Photo: Tom Carter

16. DUNDERBERG PEAK

Route: South Gully
Trailhead: Virginia Lakes
Vertical: Approx. 2,700 feet
Difficulty: Class 3
Maps: Dunderberg Peak 7.5 minute

DESCRIPTION

Dunderberg Peak is another mountain that has great ski descents on all its sides. The north side has a number of moderately steep bowls that drop down from the twin summits to Dunderberg Creek and the four-wheel drive road from Virginia Lakes. The north bowl between the summits is especially fun. The run off the southeast side to the summer cabins also is a classic descent. Of course, the bowls across the canyon are equally deserving of attention.

The route I have chosen to describe drops almost straight down to the Virginia Lakes (9,700 ft.) from the saddle between the east summit and the higher west summit (12,374 ft.). You may wish to climb straight up this gully to check out conditions, but an easier ascent takes you from the summer cabins up the southeast gully to the east summit, then down to the saddle.

Dunderberg Peak.   Photo: John Moynier

17. MATTERHORN PEAK

Route: East Couloir
Trailhead: Twin Lakes
Vertical: Approx. 4,500 feet
Difficulty: Class 4
Maps: Matterhorn Peak, Dunderberg Peak, Buckeye Ridge 7.5 minute

DESCRIPTION

Matterhorn Peak's east couloir has long been a goal of Sierra ski mountaineers. Lying in the shadow of the great north prow of the peak, this steep couloir drops straight onto the glacier. To reach the glacier, leave the trailhead at Twin Lakes (7,100 ft.) near Bridgeport, and take the Horse Creek trail up to the upper Horse Creek meadow (8,300 ft.). This broad canyon can be followed all the way up to the glacier, below the steep couloirs of Twin Peaks (12,323 ft.), or to the low saddle of Horse Creek Pass (10,700 ft.).

The route to Matterhorn Peak, however, leaves the canyon at the meadow and climbs the steep drainage to the west. The great cirque below Matterhorn Peak slowly comes into view. There are fine runs in the more moderate chutes to the east, as well as the west, of the peak. At the top of the east couloir, a short scramble takes you to the top of the peak (12,279 ft.), where you'll find a great view of the northern part of Yosemite Park, as well as the ragged Sawtooth Ridge directly to the west. After the very steep drop of the couloir, the run down Horse Creek is just good, clean fun.

Photo: John Moynier

Matterhorn Peak.

Appendix

Weather and Avalanche Information Sources

The West Side

Sequoia and Kings Canyon National Parks
Three Rivers, CA 93271
(209) 565-3306

Sierra National Forest
Pineridge Ranger District
PO Box 300
Shaver Lake, CA 93664
(209) 841-3311

Sierra National Forest
Minarets Ranger District
North Fork, CA 93643
(209) 877-2218

Superintendent
Yosemite National Park
PO Box 577
Yosemite, CA 95389
(209) 372-4232

The East Side

Inyo National Forest
Mt Whitney Ranger District
PO Box 8- S. Hwy 395
Lone Pine, CA 93545
(619) 876-5542

Inyo National Forest
White Mountain Ranger District
798 North Main Street
Bishop, CA 93514
(619) 873-4207

Inyo National Forest
Mammoth Ranger District
Hwy 203, PO Box 148
Mammoth Lakes, CA 93546
(619) 934-2505

Inyo National Forest
Mono Lake Ranger District
PO Box 10
Lee Vining, CA 93541
(619) 647-6525

Toiyabe National Forest
PO Box 595
Bridgeport, CA 93517
(619) 932-7070

Bibliography

BIBLIOGRAPHY

Avalanche Safety for Climbers and Skiers by Tony Daffern, Alpenbooks, Seattle WA, 1983.

Close Ups of the High Sierra by Norman Clyde, La Siesta Press, Glendale CA, 1976.

Free-heel Skiing by Paul Parker, Chelsea Green Publishing Co, Chelsea VT, 1988.

History of the Sierra Nevada by Francis Farquhar, UC Press, Berkeley CA, 1965.

Medicine for Mountaineering by James Wilkerson MD, The Mountaineers, Seattle WA, 1982.

Mountain Skiing by Vic Bein, The Mountaineers, Seattle WA, 1982.

Mountaineering: The Freedom of the Hills, The Mountaineers, Seattle WA, 1982.

Sierra Nevada Natural History by Storer and Usinger, UC Press, Berkeley CA, 1963.

Sierra Spring Ski-Touring by HJ Burhenne, Mountain Press, San Francisco CA, 1971.

Ski Mountaineering by Peter Cliff, Pacific Search Press, Seattle WA, 1987.

Ski Touring in California by David Beck, Pika Press, Mammoth Lakes Ca, 1980.

Ski Touring in Yosemite by Tim Messick, Chockstone Press, Denver CO, 1987.

Ski Touring the Eastern High Sierra by Don Douglass, Fine Edge Productions, Bishop CA, 1990.

Skywatch: the Western Weather Guide by Richard Keen, Fulcrum Inc, Golden CO, 1987.

The Avalanche Book by Armstrong and Williams, Fulcrum Inc, Golden CO, 1986.

The Climber's Guide to the High Sierra by Steve Roper, Sierra Club Books, San Francisco CA, 1976.

The High Route by Steve Roper, Sierra Club Books, San Francisco CA, 1980.

The John Muir Trail by Thomas Winnett, Wilderness Press, Berkeley CA, 1978.